Praise for The Hi

M000304000

"*The Hidden Gifts of Addiction* is a remarkable book—an invitation to healing, brimming with encouragement, trust, and hope. I've seldom read a book so inviting, reassuring, and hopeful. With his call to courage, Victor Bucklew continuously engages the reader with his profound compassion and offers his companionship every step of the way. He shares his personal journey and normalizes even the most painful steps in recovery.

Inspiring and uplifting, this book is destined to be a classic in the field. Yet the author's insight and wisdom are for everyone. With a deep bow of gratitude for his invaluable gift."

—OLIVIA AMES HOBLITZELLE,
author, *Aging with Wisdom: Reflections, Stories, and Teachings*

"Most of us are addicted to one thing or another, and Victor Bucklew shows us a way to healing and freedom that is grounded in self-acceptance and self-compassion. Beautifully written, this magnificent book is rich with heartfelt encouragement, soulful wisdom, and suggestions for everyday life."

—RICK HANSON, PhD,
author of *Neurodharma: New Science, Ancient Wisdom, and Seven Practices of the Highest Happiness*

"In *The Hidden Gifts of Addiction*, Victor Bucklew shares his profound wisdom about healing from addiction and what it takes to thrive in recovery. His life experience and impressive professional background combine to give the reader a heart-opening path that's both grounded and visionary. In order to heal, we must discover the hidden treasures buried in even the most painful places. Bucklew offers us the secret gems that addiction and its healing provide. Highly recommended!"

—ANA HOLUB,
addiction recovery counselor and author of *Forgive and Be Free*

"Dr. Bucklew has written a heartfelt, soulful and meditative treatise reframing addiction. Respect replaces shame, validation overrides hopelessness, and learning from suffering transforms the painful journey many people experience in recovery. Bucklew's fresh, new take on healing from addiction is a light in the darkness, long overdue."

—TESS CASTLEMAN,
LPC, Jungian Analyst, and author of *Threads, Knots, and Tapestries*

"In the first pages of this beautifully written and insightful book, Victor Bucklew speaks of his own journey with addiction: 'I gradually came to understand addiction as an unconscious resistance to what was feared or disliked in the moment.' Developing this theme, he opens up our addictive behaviors in an entirely fresh and accessible way.

"The beauty of this book is that it brings even our most destructive behaviors out of the shadows and into the light of love, kindness, curiosity, and even wonder—revealing how we can open our hearts to what is most difficult. We may find that even our darkest paths have their own kind of wisdom and gifts. Victor asks, "What if your addiction was bringing you back home to yourself and to your deepest yearning?"

"Victor invites us to ask what is really going on in this territory called 'addiction.' To pause and be with what is here—even as we are drawn to reach for something to 'fill' the moment. What is going on that feels so intolerable that we can't bear it? Is it possible to stay and feel our way into whatever is here—opening to receive the gifts that may be hidden in this very moment?"

—RICHARD WITTEMAN,
meditation teacher at Springwater Center for Meditative Inquiry

the
hidden
gifts
of
addiction

the direct path of recovery

VICTOR BUCKLEW, PhD

ROCK CREEK CANYON
PUBLISHING

Rock Creek Canyon Publishing
Richmond, VA 23235

© 2020 Victor Bucklew
All Rights Reserved
No part of this book may be used or reproduced without permission
from the author and publisher.

This book is not intended as a substitute or replacement for the medical
recommendations of physicians, mental health professionals, or other
health-care providers. Rather, it is intended to provide information and
tools for the reader to help compliment and cooperate with physicians,
mental health professionals, and health-care providers in a collaborative
quest for well-being.

Published 2020

Cover and Book Design by Rachel Valliere
Edited by Ed Levy

Printed in the United States

Library of Congress Cataloging-in-Publication Data
Name: Bucklew, Victor, 1986- author.
Title: The Hidden Gifts of Addiction: The Direct Path of Recovery /
    Victor G. Bucklew, PhD
Description: Richmond, VA : Rock Creek Canyon Publishing, [2020]
Library of Congress Control Number (LCCN): 2020921832
ISBN (papbk): 9781736043608

This book is dedicated to you and your recovery.

May you be happy, healthy, and at ease.

acknowledgments

Craig L, Jim Z, and James M, thank you for your friendship, love, and support when I needed it most.

Chelsea Muth, my wife and best friend, thank you for your tireless support throughout this project, and your help editing.

To Ed Levy, my editor, thank you for your encouragement, wisdom, and gift with the pen. This book would not have flowered without you.

contents

preface

How this book came to be

Thirteen years ago, while waking up the morning after Christmas, I heard a voice I had never heard before but which I recognized as my own. It softly told me I never needed to use heroin again. And I haven't. The voice carried the power to actualize the possibility. Even though I knew I would not use again, I did not know how I would live.

My seven-year opiate addiction and the hundreds of attempts to quit, followed by withdrawal and the inevitable relapse, had been a sort of death. I'd spent so much time living in darkness that I didn't believe there was any other way to live. When I stopped using, everything I had been numbing came to the surface.

Amidst the suffering I experienced in early recovery, I was haunted by questions about the deeper roots of my addiction, who I was without using, and if it was possible to feel peace while clean and sober.

About two years into sobriety, after persevering through 12-step programs and multiple courses of therapy, I noticed I no longer had cravings to use. But I also saw that, despite the healing I was experiencing, I had unknowingly become addicted to exercise. I wasn't able to sleep unless I vigorously exercised a few hours every day. Although exercise was healthy and important for my wellness, I was using it to numb. If I went without exercise for even a day, I felt unnerved by tremendous anxiety.

A light bulb went off: I was not using drugs any longer, yet I was not free of addiction. The healing techniques I practiced on a daily basis were helping me stay clean and sober, but the root of addiction, I now saw, lay deeper than the overt behaviors that were commonly discussed in therapy and recovery circles. I knew there had to be more to recovery and healing than sobriety.

As I continued to benefit—and to some degree continue to benefit—from both traditional and nontraditional paths of healing (12-step programs, intensive yoga practice, Western and Eastern medicine, psychotherapy, music, body and energy work, and meditation), I became increasingly fascinated with exploring addiction at its root. I intuited that if I could understand addiction on a more fundamental level, that would in itself be healing.

In this process, I came to understand addiction as an unconscious resistance to what is occurring in the present moment. I saw that addictive behavior ultimately emerged from an unseen assumption that there was a problem with the present moment that needed to be fixed before it would be okay to feel okay.

I came to see how addictive energy mixed with and contributed to so many areas of my life. It was amazing to see, even when a behavior was healthy from one perspective, how easily it could be manipulated into something else entirely when suffused with addictive energy, without my knowing. For instance, today addictive energy can appear in the quick pace that I sometimes find myself working.

Amidst a variety of experiences that I've had in recovery, including the mental gymnastics of acquiring a doctorate in ultrafast laser physics, the business-as-usual life of a government contractor, the busyness-as-usual life of a small business owner, the wonder of being a scientist researching the spooky quantum physics of light, and the love of facilitating meditation classes, there has been a turning toward rather than away from this energy.

Rather than wishing for the energy to go away, or trying to heal it away through some technique—subtle addictions in and of themselves—there has gradually developed in me an interest in compassionately meeting and being with the root energy of addiction, without strategy, or hope that it will be different. In these moments, although there is no longer a need to heal something in order to feel okay, I still at times follow healing paths—but out of pleasure and preference instead of lack and compulsion.

At such times, I feel I am living in alignment with the voice I first heard that morning after Christmas years earlier.

Deep acceptance and love for the resistance, wounding, and pain that I usually ran from reveal that health and healing are already qualities of the present moment. The addictive energy feels its connection to everything around it and no longer plays a destructive role. In fact, the energy of addiction is miraculously revealed as life energy—empowering, connecting, loving, and life affirming.

This book is an expression of a peculiar kind of inner work and recovery. As it sees addiction as a natural, unconscious process of resistance, it sees recovery as a process as well. Recovery is revealed as a loving, moment-by-moment, embrace of resistance. We do not need to wait years to feel better. Health, healing, and the peace we yearn for are in large part the life-blood of this moment. This is true even if craving and discomfort are present.

From the perspective of some contemplative traditions, this recognition might be called the "direct path" of recovery.

The chapters that follow emerged like the offering to stop using. They appeared unexpectedly one morning, thirteen years after I first heard the voice telling me I never needed to use again. The main content of the book wrote itself in less than a month. I had not intended to write it.

Who this book is for

This book is not about learning steps to follow to feel better. Rather, it is an invitation to deeply explore the inner experience of addiction while reading, and to see what emerges in the process. I would like the reader to feel welcomed, hopeful, and that they are simply being reminded of something they already know deep within themselves.

It is written primarily for people in recovery from addiction who are longing for a deeper connection with themselves and the world. It is for those who find themselves clean and sober but still feel they are missing something. It is for the reader who senses that there must have been a deeper meaning to their dance with addiction than being ripped apart and glued back together again, yet never feeling quite whole again.

While exploring common themes and challenges in recovery, the chapters also reveal the spiritual and psychological gifts residing in the midst of—and as a result of intimately being with—these challenges.

The themes and inquiries in this book are intended for someone who has been sober long enough to feel a strength of interest, and the stability, to explore the less frequently traveled and sometimes scary waters where healing, self-discovery, meaning, and peace can be revealed.

There is no prescription for how long the period of sobriety needs to be to feel that this is true for you. It may be one day or ten years. It may be never. It may be enough to simply hear, perhaps for the first time, that your dance with addiction was not in any way meaningless and that with courage, patience, interest, and honesty about your own present-moment experience, you can without a doubt discover the tremendous value and gifts that addiction has left behind for you and emerge from your addictive pattern in better shape than when you first entered it.

This book may also find its way into the hands of those who care for or counsel people struggling with addiction, or of family members or friends of people who are actively using, or in recovery. If this is you, these chapters may help you to understand the experience of your client, patient, friend, or loved one from another perspective and to also see—beyond the destruction—the gifts that the excruciating experience of addiction can leave in its wake for those willing to look.

It may also find its way into the hands of a sympathetic and interested reader who, even without being personally touched by more overt forms of addiction, cannot help but feel how compulsive, addictive behaviors are so embedded and rampant in our culture today. For such readers, it is my hope that you may discover that addiction is not just substance abuse, or gambling, etc. Addiction is not as black and white as it is portrayed. You may discover here that the energy of addiction is alive within you in various subtle ways and feel how very natural and expected this is.

To the above point, I would like to clarify my personal view of addiction, so that it may help orient the reader. To me, addiction is unconscious resistance to what is. It is everywhere in our modern, globalized world. Most of our social systems cater to behavioral patterns of numbing, resisting, and avoiding what we don't like in the present moment. Many of us are left craving, dreaming, and hyper-consuming what we do like to "fill" the present moment.

For certain people, this "filling" may take a form as overt as drug addiction. However, addiction may also be as subtle as a compulsion to repeatedly turn to thoughts to tell stories about who we are and what life is like in order to feel safe, bypassing directly being with what is happening in our present moment experience. As a result, many people feel overworked, stressed out, and unfulfilled. We need vacations after our vacations. If we are really honest, most of us will find that the core of addiction—which is presented here as a habitual and unseen resistance to what is arising for us in this moment—underlies and permeates almost our entire waking lives to some degree or another.

In my view, addiction is not something to be overcome so much as understood and loved. With love and understanding, the energy of addiction is reclaimed and can serve to profoundly enrich and enliven your experience of who you are and your felt connection with the world around you.

It is my hope that this book will guide you on a safe inquiry into how the energies of addiction are active in your life, and how natural and expected this is. I hope you will allow yourself to meet your addictive energies directly and open to a widening sense of connectedness, inwardly and with the world around you. If you begin to discover a greater sense of peace and ease, even during times of challenge and difficulty, continue to open wider. The gifts of addiction are being revealed.

How to read this book

When we open a book we expect something in return— entertainment, knowledge, or some other type of experience.

When you open a book with the intent of healing, feeling better, or deeply connecting with yourself, you may also expect to gain something. There is nothing wrong with this.

However, the question must be asked, "Is it even possible to acquire what you most yearn for?"

Some books that explore addiction, happiness, healing, and the causes of suffering speak from high places of understanding, clarity, and authority. These books often lay out very sure foundations for The Way It Is, with step-by-step instructions and practices to cultivate peace, love, and wisdom.

Sometimes, this type of writing can provide needed relief when you feel that you are at wits end and just want some instruction on how to hurt less. There is certainly value to this.

Yet, if the motivations for our reading and self-help voyages are not eventually included as part of them, our sincere attempts to heal can be hijacked and become addictions themselves. Left unchecked, the subtle movements of seeking, dependence, and avoidance remain unseen or even encouraged, providing ever-subtler ways to continue avoiding our unfaced fears.

Leading to wishes like, "If only I have that experience, or gain that insight, I will be free. Perhaps by reading these words or following those steps and trying really hard, I will be rewarded with health, healing, or at the very least, a little bit of information I can carry around with me to feel better." When we follow these threads, we usually bypass our present experience.

Although many written works may touch us deeply, the written form does not usually offer us cues to pause and explore the ever-changing parts of ourselves that appreciate and respond to the words in the first place.

When we don't pay attention inwardly, we can slip into autopilot and seek writing or information that leaves us with a sense of fullness that is—alas—not really satisfying. Generally unaware that this is happening, we ascribe our dissatisfaction to our own character—we were not paying attention closely enough, we were not trying hard enough, etc. And so we push on to the next book, or the next practice, hoping that may be the one that will magically heal us.

This process is not entirely hollow, or we wouldn't follow it. We do appear to gain short-lived insights when we momentarily relax and accept what is here. We appear to "get it." We may ascribe this to some magic in the words and try to recreate the experience or turn the insight into a prescription for the next moment—effectively covering it over, and appearing "to lose it." We can become dependent on this process. It must be asked whether the flickering light bulb of "I've got it, I've lost it" has the wattage to really warm us when it matters most.

This book invites an exploration of whether there is another way to read. It invites you to explore your present-moment experience of addiction through the process of reading, to see how deep inquiry into this alive, already present energy can lead to a freedom that is not dependent on the absence of craving or difficulty. It invites a way of reading that is not dependent on these words, or of anything that you need to learn, in order to "get it."

This book invites you to confirm in your own experience that the qualities you most yearn for have been there all along, simply waiting to be recognized. Over and over again.

My intention is not to provide you with a structure for The Way It Is. So, while reading, can you make an intention to approach the process as a simple and direct meditation—a kind of open listening?

Perhaps you will notice when clenching or resistance arises in your body when you read certain passages. If this happens, put the book down. Give yourself to the resistance. Can you see what it is like to explore it, become interested in, and perhaps even appreciate it? How curious for resistance to emerge!

And if an opening, wonder, or warmth is present, how is it that for you? How does it feel to connect with your open heart? What conditions of mind and body are present for you in these moments?

Although there is certainly a preference for feeling open-hearted, we can discover a soft joy in simply being with whatever arises, even if that whatever includes difficulty and challenging emotion.

We can let our inquiry into the deeper dimensions of addiction work on us in its own way without checking in all of the time to see how we are doing, or if we are understanding or not.

Clearly this is not a way that most of us typically read. To help facilitate this process, this book has been designed to provide space for your inner experience to emerge while you are reading. You are invited to rest in the space between paragraphs, and to discover a new rhythm and pace of reading. When we read in this way, the rhythm often fluctuates, but the pace tends to be slower than what most of us are accustomed to.

At various points, I've also inserted typographical breaks in the text, like the one here, to serve as an invitation for a longer pause. In these breaks, please feel free to put the book down, and rest in awareness of your present experience.

By working with the energies of addiction in this way, as well as learning to enjoy, create, relax, and recognize the joy in simple moments of being, we allow life to move a little bit more freely. We may be surprised at what we learn about ourselves in the process.

The goal is not to try and wrestle meaning from this book in order to feel better as an end result but to explore how we can discover a way of being with ourselves that is strangely already of peace. The words "receiving" and "inner listening" point to facets of this quality of attentive yet relaxed heart-reading and way of being that are inherently and causelessly fulfilling.

If a section does not feel relevant or resonate with your current experience, and there is no interest in being with the words or in exploring any resistance they may evoke, move on to another section or chapter and revisit that section later.

The chapters are presented sequentially, with later themes building on earlier ones, but this book may also be approached in a nonlinear way. Open the book to any chapter you feel called to, and begin there.

one

introduction

I s it possible that addiction shows up in our lives for reasons other than to decimate us and hurt those around us?

Although addiction does both of these things and more—taking lives, relationships, families, hope, and health—the havoc it wreaks might also provide a precious gift to those who are open to receiving it.

What if the destruction left in the wake of addiction is fertilizing the soil for new life—similar to the growth that inevitably follows in the aftermath of a forest fire? Besides preparing the soil for new growth, what if the suffering of addiction leaves a seed behind? Through care and attention, that seed can grow into a resilient tree capable of flourishing in the most challenging of life experiences.

Recent psychological research shows that well-being is a process, not an endpoint, similar to learning how to ride a bike or play a musical instrument. It takes practice and commitment and developing good habits, but it's also about enjoying the journey and not obsessing on results. Navigating the ups and downs, exploring the side streets, grassy lawns, and back alleys of our lives is part of what makes us human and makes us whole.

Recovery from addiction is no different. It, too, is a process.

As we explore our addictions to substances and other people, and then press inward to subtler psychological and spiritual terrains, we will usually find at the heart of addiction the same fearful clenching—a habituated and unconscious resistance to what we fear or dislike in this moment. If we are really honest with ourselves, we discover the energy of addiction almost everywhere we look. It is ingrained in some way into almost every aspect of our lives.

With this in mind, can you feel safe enough to relax a little around what is okay and what is not okay? Can you be brave enough to stop stigmatizing addiction and relax your labels around what addictive behavior is or isn't?

You can choose to look inside yourself and explore this inquiry anew. What qualities can you recognize and develop to help navigate, live with, and perhaps even find beauty in the energy of addiction within you? When you meet what has been labeled addiction in this way, is the word *addiction* still fitting? In these moments, it may seem more like you are experiencing the mysterious movement of life energy within you rather than a well-defined, separate, and scary thing called "addiction" or "craving."

The invitation to relax our labels around what addiction is or isn't is not a call to give up or a statement that the destruction left in the trail of someone who is addicted to heroin (which I once was) is the same, say, as the subtle resistance and self-clinging of a monk.

But if the unconscious resistance to what is that drives substance use disorder and other forms of addiction is the same resistance that monks go into meditation for months at a time to inquire into, doesn't the coarser expression of resistance provide a rare gift, even if no one would consciously choose it? If the root of addiction is resistance to what is, which trails an understandable misunderstanding of who we are and what we need to feel ok, there is nothing more poignant than the agony of drug addiction to help us see this and wake up to another way of being.

In this way, addiction can be a potent gift. The suffering experienced by those who have stumbled its labyrinths can open them to new possibilities. One can emerge from an addictive pattern in better shape than when they first face planted into it.

So, let us explore what inner qualities are needed to meet, trust, explore, and feel the overwhelming sensations, emotions, and thoughts that we often run to drugs, food, people, sex, work, screens, thought, or other things to cover up, numb, or mask.

Let us be patient with ourselves, knowing we will often stumble, and honor our unique process of cultivating the seed of well-being that the suffering of addiction has left inside.

There has never been anyone like you before, and there never again will be. And so, as an explorer of your own unique inner landscape of addiction, you not only provide yourself with a gift, you also afford life the beautiful opportunity to see what has never been seen before.

This is not an instruction manual. It is not a how-to guide to recovery. It is intended as a companion for you as you inquire into and explore the different facets of addiction in yourself. It is intended to introduce connections between addiction and other parts of your life that you may or may not have looked into before, to spur inquiry and question and introduce tools you might find helpful in recovery. Each chapter is a theme introducing connections between addiction and the living of this wondrous and very mysterious thing we call human life. The chapters are not comprehensive. I doubt they ever could be.

In our most direct and simplest listening, don't we know that no one (e.g., friends, family, sponsor, therapist, spiritual advisers) can give us recovery? That we cannot learn a prescribed set of steps to effectively bypass a lifetime of unprocessed and unseen emotions—even though we may have desperately hoped that we could be given a magic recipe for recovery?

Although structure and steps certainly help along the way, don't you know deep inside that there is something more to it? That you have to not only dip your toes into the waters of recovery, but eventually dive in bravely?

If we are honest, is this really a surprise?

Although this may seem scary, it is not a call to abandon reason or push yourself over the edge. It is a call to courage and a reflection that the addictions in your life are not accidents. They are not asking to be whitewashed away by a prescribed set of rules. They are far more precious than that. They are asking to be seen and explored—at your own pace. They are asking to be understood in a way that only you can really understand.

The steps and structures we often turn to in recovery are helpful as pointers or guides to direct us inward, but they are on the outskirts of town, so to speak. You must walk the path inward yourself.

Fortunately, this is not a walk where you need to toil, suffer, and beat yourself up every step along the way (even though you may start your journey doing exactly this). This is a walk that continues for the rest of your life. You never really arrive at a place where it all ends.

Does this reflection depress you? Does it bring up fear?

Let me be clear. This walk never ends because this process of life never ends. Your recovery is a process because life itself is a process. You are being held in each and every moment by life itself. It may be challenging, and the scenery may change and become more pleasant, but it always continues. Can you find a way to let this help you relax more? To be more patient and forgiving with yourself? To be more understanding? More loving?

Can you let this reflection help you feel safe enough to open to a wonder and curiosity that are already here? Can you see what this moment is like, knowing that it won't arise again in the same way?

There is freedom in this recognition.

There is freedom in knowing that your happiness and well-being cannot be obtained down the road after you somehow make it through this muddy patch. In this seeing, there is a possibility that this moment can be appreciated. Not because you enjoy or necessarily appreciate what is happening but simply because it is here. Because it has already been welcomed and allowed here before any judgments or stories about its goodness or badness have even had time to arise. And inescapably, because judgmental stories that can cause so much pain also belong here. They too have been welcomed, along with the tension they often drag in their wake.

In this seeing, isn't there a possibility that the muddy patch where our shoes are now stuck and into which we have now face planted again is, from a certain perspective, perfectly placed and meaningful?

Tell me, how would the inner landscapes of fear, trauma, mistrust, grief, sadness, confusion, and overwhelm appear if their labels were dropped—or at least seen as labels— and the sensations were experienced directly? Would they appear fundamentally any different than the vistas afforded by rolling mountain foothills?

☀

Let us explore our addictions together. Let us explore suffering. Pain. Grief. Despair. Confusion. Fear. Not because it is the right thing to do, but because it is the only thing to do. If the energies of addiction and the emotional, physical, and mental storms they brew are present in your life right now, what are they asking for? What is asking to be seen? How can you learn to live again? How can you learn to be in relationship and to gradually and gently work with trauma? How can you begin to feel and welcome what has been historically rejected?

Addiction requires you to face it all. It demands that you honestly and courageously—which doesn't require the absence of fear—look inside and out to see where you are. Addiction asks you to attune to your deepest yearning. Again and again. For only this deepest yearning— which may be to feel safe, peaceful, loved, or connected deeply with oneself, one's family, one's community, or spirituality—has a sturdy enough sail to weather the harsh winds of addiction.

What is your deepest yearning?

It is okay if this is not clear or known right now. This is not a setback. Sometimes our deepest yearning cannot be articulated, and more often than not we are the last ones to know. It also seems as though it is always expressing itself a little bit differently than the last time we were aware of it. When we are honest, doesn't our deepest yearning point more to an integrated, connected, present-moment process, than a fixed end point? Doesn't it tug us gently towards a grounded sober love that can only be felt right here, in this moment?

There is no need to force anything. Your yearning may take time to surface. It may percolate to the surface in a dream, artistic creation, or desperate prayer. It may surprise you by revealing itself in the midst of struggle, torment, tension, and the feeling of rottenness. You might find it right in the midst of the mundane. Or maybe even in these words.

Your conscious mind may feel fearful to admit or articulate what you most yearn for in your heart. Is it true that addiction is both a response to and turning away from this fear? It can feel vulnerable to share your deepest yearnings. It can feel as though, if you give them voice, they could be wiped away, leaving nothing left to hold your life together. You may be right, and this may not be such a bad thing.

But tread gently.

Know that what you yearn for is present and healthy, and waiting to be embraced, loved, recognized, and realized.

Can you host the question, "What if my addictions were bringing me back home to myself and to my deepest yearning?"

What if, through intimacy with the energies of addiction, you found that these energies hadn't robbed you of yourself but all along, perhaps unskillfully and foggily, had been trying to call you home in the only way that they knew how?

Wouldn't this change everything?

two

the mystery of healing

How much control do we actually have over healing?
This can be a scary question. However, a deep and honest
inquiry can reveal so much.

You have a unique path of healing, and so there is no need
to look outward or compare yourself to others.

I'm willing to bet that how you came or will come to sobriety is as unique and mysterious a process as every other
part of your path of addiction and recovery.

Although simply not using isn't enough to be free from
what you were trying so desperately to numb, it is a cru-
cially important step in the process.

I have known people who stopped using for the last time
after years of cycling in and out of treatment centers and
recovery groups. One day, something finally stuck. Nothing
changed, yet at the same time, everything changed. I have

seen others who stopped using after life-threatening illness turned them upside down. I know someone who woke up and stopped using by going to prison. And another friend who needed to go through treatment only once—where family intervention really worked. Another friend eventually stopped using very gradually. This friend got medicine to help with the physical withdrawals and then gradually just became more interested in living life, being in relationship, and working a satisfying career than using.

For myself, I remember lying in bed the morning after Christmas thirteen years ago and hearing a voice that I had never heard before. It said, "You never need to use again." And I haven't. The authority and strength in that voice carried with it the support needed to actualize the possibility.

That voice emerged after trying to quit hundreds of times over the preceding four years. I would stop using and then be almost totally bedridden from withdrawal for the next few days. During these days, I was utterly consumed by strong emotional, physiological, and psychological craving. I would fluishly shake. I wanted to die. After three or four days of this, just before breaking the worst of the withdrawals, I would inevitably relapse. I would fall back into the hole with more self-disgust, despair, and hopelessness than before. For four years, this process continued over and over again.

When the voice emerged, I had been living at home for about a month trying to get by. Both of my parents knew. It was all out in the open. After leaving the state and trying to escape my opiate addiction by relocating, I had come back home and relapsed within the first two weeks of being there.

Would I have even heard the voice and been willing to trust it if I hadn't relapsed so often? I will never know. However, I suspect that all of the relapses and suffering were needed for me to really hear and take heed of those words.

It is important to note that the morning after I heard this voice, I didn't magically feel healed, cured, or free from addiction.

Not at all.

However, a sense of choice was presented that I had never felt before. With the choice came the power and energy to follow through. It was no longer a question for me. I knew that I would not use again, although I didn't know how I would live with myself.

I looked everywhere for the answer to that. I went to outpatient therapy twice a week. I saw an individual counselor. I saw another counselor at the methadone clinic I was going to at the time. I went to two or more AA meetings a day for the first year and a half of sobriety.

I put in a lot of work.

I became addicted to sobriety, to being clean. I found new friends and discovered a new community. I worked the steps. I volunteered at a local clubhouse. I found a sponsor and also sponsored. I marked each day clean with a big X on a calendar that I kept on the wall of my room. Below the X, I tracked my number of days without using. Above the X, I kept track of the meetings I had attended that day. One day at a time, I began to confront my fears. For the first time that I could remember, I experienced the value of money as more than just how many drugs it could buy. I experienced anxiety and emotions I had never consciously felt before. A lot of anxiety. A lot of pain. I started a new relationship that was not centered around drugs or using. I awkwardly hung out with new friends in recovery. None of us knew what to say or do with ourselves. Life was awkward. It was a process of learning how to live and be in the world again.

This process continues in different forms today. I don't see how it could end. Almost all of us are addicted to something. We are all masking something or running away from some emotion, thought, or story that we are afraid will bury us. Some of us do this in more overt and destructive ways than others.

What I learned and continue to learn through this process is that healing is a very mysterious thing. Can I point to a specific moment when healing began? Did it begin when that voice mysteriously entered the room the morning after Christmas? Why not the first time I tried to quit?

What about for you?

When did you begin to heal?

If you are really honest with yourself, haven't you already begun, even if things don't look so great right now?

When we consider that our efforts to heal matter so much and yet not at all, we allow ourselves to relax more. We find that we don't need to take ourselves so seriously. We may also find that our resolution to recover is empowered in a way that it can never be while we are fearfully hanging on and trying to manage every aspect of our inner and outer lives. When we see that we don't know what will come tomorrow, or if tomorrow will come at all, we open to the possibility of wonder, humility, and the willingness to look anew.

Often, we hear that we need to hit rock bottom in order to heal. We hear that we do a disservice to ourselves, or to the one struggling with addiction, by preventing this hitting of bottom.

What is this pointing to?

Does it really mean we need to let everything fall apart before we can start to heal and climb out of the pit we have dug ourselves into? What if hitting bottom points more to an attitude than a fixed event? What if one quality of this attitude is that we see how we are in control in certain ways and yet not at all in even more ways—that we are changing and growing processes.

This attitude seems to come about through a certain kind of dying. When we hit bottom, we realize that all of our strategies, attempts, and maneuvers to not hurt so damn much have failed miserably.

It allows us to laugh more, not take ourselves so seriously.

Although we had managed to escape consciously feeling our pain for a while, it was patiently waiting for us the whole time. Waiting for us to muster the courage to really feel.

In these darkest moments, we let go a little. We allow a part of ourselves to die, the part that thought that it could really figure it out. That it could somehow keep away and perpetually numb the rivers of shame, torment, and suffering winding through us.

With this recognition, you may feel that you are submerged and swimming in emotion. You may find yourself struggling to breathe but at the same time watching everything simply unfold—looking sometimes like a movie and sometimes like a train wreck. You realize in these moments that although you are at the bottom of the barrel, it is just where you belong. You realize that there isn't much to do besides simply see and be there totally.

To be totally out of options.

Perhaps the most sincere place one can ever be.

From this place strength emerges.

From this place, the submerged, struggling, now slightly humbled personality can begin to act and make decisions that are not wholly based on escaping this moment.

Through no action of our own, the personality sees that it just doesn't work. With this, we grudgingly begin to face our experiences in this moment. We realize there is nothing we can ever escape and that the kindest thing we can do for ourselves is to simply be here with and in whatever arises.

This is a humbling process.

You may feel as if your mind is unraveling. You may find yourself crying all the time. You may feel isolated. And that no one understands you.

This is all so normal.

These voices that have been repressed for so long are finally being allowed to come out of the shadows and be heard.

Their screams may not be pretty, but they are absolutely expected. Through finally meeting our inner experiences with honesty and love, we can notice a sense of ourselves that is deeper than any story, emotion, or thought that we may be having. We can notice whether the part that has let go has opened up space for recognizing what has always been here. And once opened, the connection with the presence of this moment, a deeper aspect of who we are, always remains. All of us have let go in some way, by simply being here embodied—even if this connection to life appears to be closed and we seem to be hitting our heads endlessly against the walls in frustration.

In the open wake of letting go and saying yes to this moment, can we recognize ourselves?

Can we see that even difficulty, shame, fear, and guilt are alright?

This space that appears to emerge is the result of letting go of the belief that we can somehow control life and make it better for ourselves if we just try a little bit harder.

This is one of the gifts of addiction.

Addiction pushes us to a point where our outer strategies for numbing become just as excruciatingly painful as the inner suffering we are trying to avoid or run away from. In between these pressures, the part of ourselves that thought it could somehow figure it all out collapses. It dies a little. And then the bottle is uncorked and it all comes out.

Although the part of us suffering from addiction might like this to be a cathartic experience or the ultimate high, can we relax around what this should look like? Sometimes this process happens gradually, each relapse eating away at the sense of control little by little. Sometimes it happens in one fell swoop. We really don't know how it will happen for us.

With this in mind, you may notice that it feels just a little bit safer to simply listen to your own present moment experience and not be so worried about what healing might look like for you as an end goal.

Wouldn't you feel freer in this moment if you could see that it is the only moment you ever really have?

※

You may find that it is a little bit easier to relax around what it means to heal, and whether or not you are in charge and "doing" it correctly. You may pleasantly find that the permission to simply relax into an intimacy with this moment is inherently healing. You may realize this is the only place healing can ever occur and also the only place where—in a way—you feel already healed and at peace by simply being.

※

Although our intentions and actions matter so much (they really do), we are just one small part of life. We are just one part and process of a larger collection of energetic processes that we are held within.

Do you make your heart beat?

Do you move the breath in and out of your body?

Thank goodness the conscious mind and personality are not in control of everything. How limiting the experience of life would be if we needed to consciously beat our heart. Could we even do it? A friend once said to me, "With our attention spans, we would probably forget or get distracted, and that would be the end of it!" What a mystery this process of life is!

If we look outside ourselves, don't we see that the processes of healing and growth are intimately intertwined with the processes of destruction? Could it be any other way inside this human body and mind? Aren't we connected to life in the same way that a plant is?

Destruction often clears the way for something new to emerge. New seedlings grow from the rot of dead and decaying, once majestic and kingly trees. Let us not be too hasty to judge our "failures" and "setbacks," for we don't know what fertilizer they might serve as for some new seed of wellness. In fact, we can be certain that in the wake of destruction, new life will grow.

We just don't know how, when, or what form it may take. With this in mind, is it possible to simply enjoy the process, do our best, and keep on keeping on?

three

what is addiction asking for?

Two important questions to ask about addiction are "What frightening emotions are your addictive behaviors covering up and numbing for you?" and "What would be needed for both yourself and these frightening emotions to feel safe and cared for?"

⁂

When the energy of addiction emerges, our normal response is either to give in to what we think will satisfy it or to push it away. We label and categorize the energy and then assign interventions to get rid of it. The energy of addiction is mostly considered a disease, affliction, or character defect. As something to be covered up, ashamed of, repressed, healed, contained, minimized, or fixed.

Do these attitudes toward addiction reflect wisdom or fear?

Isn't the fixation on the absence of addiction another addiction?

So much of the power of addiction lies in our personal and collective relationship to it. When we respond from fear of being taken over, swallowed up, or relapsing, we close ourselves off to the possibility of learning something new.

We dissociate from our actual experience and enter the stale, though apparently safer, world of formulaic ideas about what addiction is or isn't, what is healthy and what isn't, and what needs doing to "get back on track." Is it any surprise that recovery rates are so low? By working with addictive energy using only the crude tools of modern consumer life—overpowering, outcompeting, and over-coming—we give our power away and obscure our own wisdom, as well as the wisdom of addiction.

We do not recover from addiction by overpowering it and beating it into a state of submission. In certain cases, with these approaches addiction energy may modulate into less overt and destructive forms, but without learning to feel, love, and embrace what our addictive behaviors were lov-ingly but unconsciously numbing for us, the energy of addiction remains unseen and plays destructive roles in our lives.

Of course it is like this.

By not becoming interested in our addictions and what they are pointing to in our lives—right here and now—we close ourselves off from the wisdom in this moment. We reduce, categorize, and label perfectly unique movements of life as "cravings, relapses, addictions, or problems" as though we have understood them. In doing so, we miss seeing addiction as an all-pervading quality of modern life affecting us all.

Although labeling can help when approaching something we are scared of, we ultimately need to do much better. Labeling from a safe mental distance does not help us intimately touch the addictive energies inside us. At best, labeling can get us into the same room with addiction energy.

The usually unseen resistive energy of addiction is also not touched by correcting and changing our behaviors. Although techniques of behavioral therapy and the life-styles we follow are indispensable tools of living healthier lives, they don't get to the core of addiction. Although they can buy space and time for us to feel safe enough to approach emotions that once scared us so much we felt we needed to numb, they do not replace genuinely feeling and becoming intimate with these emotions.

23

More than asking what you need to do to heal your addictions to get "back on track," what would it be like to hang out with them for a while? What would it be like to explore the contours, shapes, and movements of addictive energy within?

☀

Addictive energies are not only negative and destructive, they are also creative, cunning, and at times ecstatic. No addiction is the same. No message is the same.

Addictive energy underlies almost every part of our personal and collective lives. Most of the time we delude ourselves into thinking we have done away with addiction. Usually, we are just pushing water around. The energy remains, and more often than not we don't learn very much from the effort. We don't really listen.

Addiction remains and is present because it is asking to share its message and to express itself. It is not asking to be silenced or fixed. Like everything else in our lives, addiction is asking to be deeply listened to.

☀

The message addiction may share does not need to be profound. It does not need to be some big revelation. You don't even need to learn some new piece of information about yourself that you can carry with you to somehow help make sense of your life and hurt less.

The message of addiction is often subtler than that. It is connected with this moment and everything happening in it and disappears just as soon as it emerges. It is always speaking in new, never before heard words. It is less about searching for meaning and trying to listen to something in particular and more about opening to the wonder of this very moment.

Your connection with the qualities of wonder and acceptance allow both the space and intimacy needed to make your meetings with addiction safe, loving, and trusted (even if there is also fear, mistrust, and anger present).

∗

When you do not conflate your addictive behavior of choice with the usually unseen resistance that *is* addiction, how do you experience addiction? What is it like to viscerally attune to the habitual energy of resistance inside you that *is* addiction? What do you discover?

∗

What traumatic stories of the past or squashed hopes for the future might be whispered to you? Through moment-by-moment, awake, visceral embrace of inner resistance, what if you were to discover hidden yearnings and callings? A cry to follow a new career path, for instance. A desire to play the instrument you never had the time to take up. A longing to reestablish an old friendship. To mourn an ending you were previously unable to.

In the dark places inside where you turn to drugs, people, or things to mask, distract, and cover up, what do you find? Recovery from addiction is not so much a process of getting rid of something as of developing the courage to become intimate with the places inside you have not felt safe enough to be with before. It is to awaken fully to the myriad of ways that we all habitually resist aspects of what is. This kind of awakening is a process, even if it does sometimes clearly articulate itself in memorable 'aha' moments.

⁂

Awakening to the presence of resistance does not mean that resistance will necessarily disappear. It just means that in the moment you see that resistance is not a problem. It is a natural pattern of life, and its emergence no longer divides you or your life into separate things. While distinctions of course still remain, when this moment is not being divided into essentially separate pieces, is there anything really that requires numbing?

⁂

The darkness and suffering tied into addiction are so profound and acute that they demand a very strong medicine to silence. It makes sense that we resist what is painful, and prefer what is pleasurable. There is nothing wrong with this. However, when we fall asleep to the ways that we resist, and then set up like and dislike relationships with life, we feel like we literally *are* resistance. Don't you often feel solid, fixed, and right at the center of it all? How many of the qualities of who you feel yourself to be have been conflated with the qualities of habituated unconscious resistance?

※

Make no mistake. We all have places of darkness that we have at one time or another turned away from. By turning to these places and embracing our darkness, what might we learn? Is it possible that we might grow in the process? Isn't there a certain creative fertility in the dark?

Don't your primal, terrorized screams hide something very connective? Spiritual almost? What if you began to develop an intimacy with all that you had rejected?

※

One of the gifts of addiction is that through this process we become larger. Although our darkness demands that we face it, to a degree it is our choice how we respond to its call. In this process, we gradually become less self-involved. Not because we are saints but because it is an evolutionary necessity. Evolve or die. And as we learn to become more intimate with our own suffering and darkness, we can also be more present with the suffering and darkness in others.

Through your suffering and your courage to meet what has been previously masked, you open yourself to new possibilities as a person, partner, friend, and member of this wounded and hurting collective. Please honor and appreciate this oftentimes horribly painful process of developing intimacy with what once was disowned. Know that others may not understand your inner experiences, or your courage, or the suffering that you may often experience, but that all involved will benefit from your work. It may be silent work that does not produce a diploma, but it is precious and valuable, and its fruits will stay with you the rest of your life.

Yet, it does not end. There is no arrival point where darkness has somehow been totally seen and transmuted into light—one of our favorite societal bypasses.

Darkness seems to mostly remain dark.

What does seem to change is the power that it holds over us. Instead of motivating fear (and using drugs or other addictions to cover this up), it can inspire creative work. It can provide the welcoming foundation to invite others to their own work. Most importantly, it can be a homecoming, as you recognize yourself in aspects of life that you had previously shunned and were thus restricted and limited by. You are given the gift of freedom from the prisons of goodness, properness, and light. Which lets you land here barefoot in this moment with dirt under your toenails.

What changes is that the rawness of darkness can reflect a kind of beauty. And once you can notice the beauty in darkness, you are free of its hold upon you.

So, let us continue to explore what our addictions are asking for. What are they pointing to? What have we disowned about ourselves that is asking to be seen?

This process may be challenging, but know that it is a homecoming and that those parts of you that may fall away are not fundamental. It is also a process of growth. Yet, paradoxically, it is also about recognizing within you that which does not require growth.

This full-blooded embodied intimacy with addiction is sacred. Can you dare to approach it with the attitude of reverence that it deserves?

four

your unique path

Each of the stories of how we become addicted, how the addiction plays out, and how we begin to heal is unique. I don't think I've heard a story that is exactly the same as any other.

This is a beautiful thing.

The very particular way that your mind, body, and spirit touch the heartbreaking suffering, excruciating craving, and miserable withdrawal involved in your dance with addiction is beautiful from a certain perspective.

Although addiction feels anything but beautiful when we are unconsciously in the midst of it, can we explore this possibility when we are feeling less overwhelmed to see if it holds any value?

One of the tremendous possibilities always open to us is to come closer and closer to seeing and touching what is happening right now.

Whatever that may be.

Even if you are lost in cycles of trauma or craving, can you cultivate an intimacy with your experience and, besides feeling bogged down, overwhelmed, disassociated, or ungrounded, know that somewhere in the background and almost off-screen that it is all right?

Can you notice not only the content of what is unfolding in front of your eyes but also the essential qualities of that content? Can you see that the particular psychosomatic sensations that comprise this moment disappear as soon as they arise, only to be replaced by new (even if apparently similar) sensational landscapes? Can you notice the qualities of movement and change that underlie every experience?

These questions invite an exploration of whether it is possible to be simultaneously intimate with different layers of your experience. In a way, this is not dissimilar to how you might admire a work of art. You may appreciate the brushstrokes of paint on canvas while also taking in and enjoying the landscape created from the textured globs of paint. Or, you may cringe at a hellish picture in front of you but still appreciate the masterful skill that birthed such an intense emotional response. And at the same time, regardless of what you are seeing, there is also a totally natural, nonconceptual knowing of who you are, a knowing presence that lovingly welcomes each and every moment—whether the familiar impression of who you seem to be appears or not.

※

When we look closely, we may intuit that this loving presence is actually more fundamental than the sense of our being fundamentally separate people.

※

In somewhat of a paradox, we connect with presence—the essence of this present moment— through a spontaneous and ever fresh realization that tells us life has always been this way, even though it feels we are discovering it for the first time.

※

In this way, even difficulty can become an opportunity to wonder. And when we are open and more curious about the nature of what is occurring than whether it is okay or not, we open to the possibility of more skillfully responding to the circumstances of our lives.

This kind of seeing does not preclude action, and it certainly does not make you a doormat for others to wipe their feet on. There is tremendous courage involved in seeing the whole picture—content and essence, inner and outer—which imbues one with the freedom to respond. This freedom is not so much a matter of being able to choose a path forward in a hostile world you are trying to navigate. Rather, this freedom is paradoxically one in which personal choice is driven by the whole of life itself. In this way, freedom is more of a life-wide choice that simply is the next movement of it all.

When we are not stuck in cycles of thought, we can see these cycles as intricate patterns unfolding within us, and that gives us more freedom to respond creatively. This freedom doesn't mean giving up healthy boundaries. We simply no longer require that life should look or feel a certain way. We see that we really don't have as much control over life as we once thought.

We also find that we have much more freedom than we ever thought.

Doesn't the need to control ultimately stem from the yearning for freedom? What if freedom was more accessible to you through letting go of the need to control this moment, and attuning to gratitude that this moment is here at all? This is not something to be taken on faith. It is presented as a question to explore within your own experience.

Right now, reading these words, can you notice a part of yourself that is already free? A part that touches, connects with, and is the awareness that allows the sensations dancing on the surface of this page to organize into worded waves of perception. You may discover that this kind of noticing results from spontaneously letting go and trusting what is here.

This moment-by-moment letting go is a letting go into who you have always been. Aware. This is a letting go into wakefulness.

While exploring addiction, can you become interested in the difficult aspects, the challenging emotions, and the crippling thoughts? Can you somehow see the beauty in them? If not in the content, can you see that they are pieces of life that are moving, spinning, and alive, just like everything else? Can you find a certain beauty in that?

No one can do this for you.

As this moment has never before arisen in exactly the same way, no one could possibly provide you with a recipe for meeting it.

If we consider that addiction is a turning away from our present experience, and toward what appears to numb, distract, or erase what we fear we cannot face—what might we learn about healing from addiction?

If healing from addiction is learning to face and dance with the inner darkness and wounded places we have disowned, covered up, and tried to run far away from, could there ever be any other place or time to heal than right here and right now? Where else but in this sensational moment could we ever learn to dance?

Is there anyone else in the world besides you who could possibly know what you are experiencing right now?

Isn't it so totally unique?

The beauty is that you can't get it wrong! How could you? There is nothing by which you could measure this moment because it has never happened before.

Ever!

As you turn inward, relax around what the outcome should be. Relax judgments around what you think you should feel, and whether or not you are doing it right.

Not because you should try to do nothing but because you really can't bring anything with you into this moment from your own memory or from someone else's experience that could adequately prepare you for this.

⁂

This moment is perfectly new and unique, even if thought says, "What's so unique and new about jumping onto this filthy bus at 5:30 am every morning to get my methadone dose so I can stop withdrawing and get some sleep?"

That is a thought that is describing experience. An unhappy one. And a natural and expected one.

It is an interpretation designed to apparently help navigate this moment easier.

This is completely normal. If it is here, it belongs here.

Why?

Because, it could not possibly be any other way than how it is right now. This is its rightful and natural home. For now. You also have your rightful and natural home in this moment, just as your resistance does. All of it perfectly belongs. Through this acceptance of both the "me" that is resisting and the feeling, thought, or sensation that is being resisted, what is seen?

Doesn't a certain space open up?

Isn't it curious that this knowing space is holding all of it?

Isn't it always?

From here, you are just a changing pattern within it, a pattern not unlike that resisted sensation that is perhaps now just a little different. Your fear is also held here. And perfectly belongs. And your joy, of course, as well. What is it like to rest here and make this open space of being—of seeing—your home?

As we rest here—in present seeing—what is it like to explore the thinking mind?

Categorizing and labeling help with daily tasks of life—for instance, in learning to drive a car. It's good that we don't need to try to remember where the brake and accelerator are each time we get into the car. Through listening, thinking, concentrating, and practice, much of the activity of driving has become unconscious activity.

This is normal. We can see only so much at one time. These unconscious labels, assumptions, and habits help us navigate the complex tasks of our daily lives. These unconscious patterns provide structure for new conscious material to play out upon. New layers of experience can emerge from intimacy and familiarity with other layers.

Unconscious processes keep us alive. But what if they also cause a lot of unnecessary pain? For instance, what about the unconscious thought process that thinks it has seen the way it is in this moment, quickly draws some conclusion, and automatically acts accordingly? What effect does the assumption that there is nothing noteworthy about this moment have on our experience?

Where did we learn it?

Is it true?

☀

Unconscious patterns of memory are beautiful and amazing when they reflect something that has been welcomed and thoroughly digested. These patterns help enrich the experience of this moment.

However, when unconscious patterns emerge from some previous moment that was shunned and numbed, they cause a lot of pain. Thought is potent and creates a literal experience for us from its content, even if that content is not reflective of the way something is in this moment.

It hurts when our thoughts or perspectives are not reflective of how things are. It hurts even more when these thoughts remain unseen, unquestioned and become the background assumptions we use to navigate through life.

Unconscious patterns—which will always be part of our experience—contribute to the richness of our lives when they enable the space and material for consciousness to flower in this moment. For instance, the unconscious processes of breathing and the pumping of blood in and out of the heart allow us to take in and feel the diversity of sense experience in a very rich way.

Regardless of what our unconscious patterns are doing, we cannot throw them away. We can, however, try to become aware of and interested in them, notice their movements, and welcome them wholeheartedly into our present experience. When we actively welcome the discomfort of unpleasant and limiting unconscious patterns in this way, we discover that these patterns no longer contribute so strongly to the feeling of being an unhappy, scared person hiding somewhere behind the eyes. Rather, we discover that our radical welcoming seeps into the cells of our bodies and reveals itself as an energetic healing aliveness that is inseparable from the wounds, bruises, and fractures that it may often caress.

Just as water flows through a canyon creek, the fresh and creative waters of the present moment mix with and are directed by memory—which stands upright and apparently fixed, just like canyon walls. The question is, is memory enriching or degrading our experience? When we are perched atop canyon walls of memory, looking down at our experience from long distant mental views, it all looks the same. We may see that there is water, and that the water is moving, but we are not close enough to notice the particulars. Moreover, we are not interested in the particulars. We feel like we have seen water moving through the canyon beneath us for as long as we can remember. It is not interesting. Living like this, we feel trapped in our memories.

However, when we are submerged within the waters and spontaneity of the moment, we can miss out on the perspective afforded by the canyon walls. We can miss out on seeing that even though the water is moving and turning in new ways, it is also impacted by the historically shaped edges of the canyon walls. Both are present in each and every moment. Both impact our experience.

Can we see, acknowledge, and appreciate both?

What wisdom arises for you when you honor that your present experience is in part dictated by the past but is also completely new and has never been seen before?

If you see craving arise, can you know that this is perfectly okay? Although craving tends to gradually diminish and eventually dissolve over time, it makes perfect sense that it might arise in early recovery. Becoming aware of its presence is a sign that you are more aware of the natural patterns and expressions of life within you. It may be unpleasant, but this is the path of freedom. Given your history with addiction, it is absolutely expected and healthy for patterns of craving to emerge. How else could it really be?

However, alongside this acceptance, based on a present clear seeing of the impact of history and memory, can you also notice that *this* craving is a little different?

41

What it is like when you drop the label *craving* as the final truth of your experience and dare to include it alongside the completely mysterious, sensational twists, turns, and movements of this alive and present energy inside you now? The felt experience of pulling, clenching, stagnation, and disorientation that is new but also understood as meaningfully tied to your unique history with addiction.

Through this multi-layered intimacy with your experience of craving, where you are not fixated on any one particular aspect of it, can you see that a part of who you are is free?

Can you feel that your present experience is perfectly acceptable, and could not be any other way based on your past? Can you see that the form it now takes is totally new? Doesn't this seeing diminish identification with the miserable suffering "me" from a certain perspective?

Then, you may become so intimate with the experience that you are both witnessing it and completely present and in touch with it from within the swirling, embodied, and energetic movements that it takes. It becomes harder to find your own edges, even as boundaries and distinction help enrich your experience.

In order to be truly intimate with life, we need to first realize who we are not. This can feel like a scary process of emptying. However, at a point, this emptying becomes so full. It becomes the fullness of being. Witnessing from ever-subtler states of mind gives way to a seeing-being who is within and intimately connected, not dissociated or disconnected, from every moment.

It seems like this journey of abstraction and questioning—wondering who or what we really are—and what truth is—is necessary, until it, too, is seen as a movement within it all.

It too can be lovingly held within this moment, when life awakens to see that wondering, questioning, and looking are aspects of itself. And have always been so.

It is a great joy to discover that only you can track, nurture, love, and be the totally unique and winding process of life that you so perfectly are.

five

addiction and
the body

I n the context of healing addiction, the body is often
treated as a kind of sewage system for the mind.

The mind is thought to be the place where the real work
takes place, and the body is considered some kind of secondary vessel that at best is there to sustain or support
the mental process of healing. Although there is sometimes a nod to the importance of feeding the body good
food, exercising it, and potentially drugging it to alleviate
unfavorable symptoms of craving or pain, it is usually not
treated as a wildly intelligent participant in the healing
of addiction. It is rarely turned to for wisdom or direction. Although there are certainly some alternative recovery
modalities that do look to the body for direction, more
often than not, in the mainstream of addiction treatment,
the body is treated like a pet animal that is doing its job if
it stays out of the way and behaves.

From this mainstream perspective, it may seem strange to dedicate a chapter to the role of the body in healing addiction. However, addictive behavior so often emerges as a result of fearfully and unconsciously turning away from the sensational messages and wisdom of your body.

Perhaps you fear that meeting intense physical pain in your body will amplify it and make you unable to do anything. Or perhaps there are deep emotional wounds that you fear might swallow you whole, leaving nothing behind but an unlovable mess. Maybe you are inundated by unbearably negative and continuous thought—mental sensations that won't pause long enough to let you take a breath. Under the pressure of these strong energies, many of us turned to addiction to numb, cope, and feel a little better.

We numbed until our methods of coping were as painful as the inner environments we had run away from in the first place.

As we come back in touch with our bodies—at our own pace—exercise can be very helpful. Yoga, running, boxing, massage, and team sports can help. Don't expect your mind to appreciate this offering as much as your body will. It's easy to know this at an intellectual level—but at an embodied level, it is chemically transformative when your body starts moving.

You can turn to these activities not only for enjoyment but also for re-familiarizing yourself with this physical home of yours that you may not have cleaned, flushed, or dusted for years. If ever.

When you stop using, the emotional, mental, and sensational aftermath is challenging. It can go on for years. This
is expected. And natural. Doesn't it make sense?

Although you may have secretly hoped that ignoring the
most disliked or scary parts of yourself would make them
go away, this strategy never really pans out.

The persistence of the body's wisdom—which asks that
we embrace what has been given us—is actually quite
beautiful.

The body lovingly stores the shadows of our past that
we cannot bear to face—until it's safe. I have had experiences of old images, sensations, tastes, even patterns
of body movement return during sessions with trusted
bodyworkers.

By developing an intimacy with the body—which we need
to do slowly, with guidance and with care for ourselves—
the mysterious, beautiful, and wise organism will often
begin to speak.

The body speaks in a different language than the conscious
mind. What we are labeling "the body" has different memories than the conscious mind. Sometimes the body holds
memory of events the conscious mind never even per-
ceived. Embodied memory is much more than a simple
recording apparatus. The body also registers, enjoys, and
enriches this moment in ways the mind can only imagine.
It is a portal through which we can contact and be moved

by the intelligent presence of life that is the basis for each and every moment.

☀

The ability of the body to hold overwhelming sensation for us until we can meet it plays an important role in releasing addictive patterns.

For instance, once, during a bodywork session, everything in the room went black, and I felt a sharp pain in my right arm. It was right where I used to stick needles. It appeared as though something black shot out of it. Like poisoned blood. I don't know what it was, but the person working with me also felt it.

Later, a memory emerged: the arm swelling up after shooting up with a dirty needle and thinking I would need to go to the hospital. I had not consciously thought about it since it happened years earlier. I certainly didn't contrive the memory. The body was holding it there for me. When my arm swelled up, I felt terrified and shut down. I thought I might lose my arm, that I had poisoned myself, that I might die. I was ashamed and scared. After the swelling went down on its own, I pushed the event out of mind. However, the unprocessed overwhelm and alarm in my body was lovingly held until I could feel it during that session.

Although memory doesn't always do the ever-fresh and creative expression of life justice, it is one way the body expresses its reverence for the life which beats its heart and draws it breath, even if the conscious mind was unable to connect at that past time when the memory was "created."

You are not free of an emotion just because you succeed in pushing it out of or displacing it from your conscious mind. You may succeed in pushing it so far down that your conscious mind no longer needs to directly confront it, but the energy of the emotion remains in, and continues to influence, your body, nervous system, and mind until it can be seen. There are many ways something can be seen, but consciously working with these emotions is one of the most direct.

These emotions are not held in the body to punish you. They remain because... how else could it be? Doesn't everything leave some trace of memory in its wake?

☀

This is true everywhere we look in nature. In the soil we find memory of trees. In the streams flow distant memories of great thunderheads. In sunlight hides memory of fusion reactions that took place nearly one hundred million miles away in the center of the sun.

Wouldn't it make sense that everything you have ever experienced would also leave a memory or trace behind inside of you? Aren't we all little modulations of nature?

Everything that happens has an impact. Processes seem to change when they are met by another process or given the space to breathe and take new form. When we push something down, that process remains, just in a contracted way and out of sight. It contributes to the composition of the soil of your physical, emotional, and psychological life. If you want to change the composition of the soil, you need to let those seeds you have pushed down grow, bloom, be appreciated, and perhaps pruned, redirected, starved, or even buried. You do not know what the appropriate response will be until you have watched the petals of that once-shunned black flower ripple in the moonlight winds of your consciousness.

In another instance, while a practitioner was working on my neck, visceral images of being thrown around like a rag doll from the impact of a ski accident emerged. I had broken my neck eleven years earlier, and the unprocessed sensations and images were still inside.

There is sometimes a tremendous energetic component to these viscerally felt images. There can also be a strong emotional component. We might cry afterward.

Isn't it beautiful that we can connect with parts of ourselves that we were unable to before? We may sense sometimes that, despite feeling devastated, nothing is ever really lost.

A therapist or spiritual friend may be helpful during these periods. To assure us that we really are okay and that this is a natural process. To help us see for ourselves that although it may feel overwhelming, these visceral sensations are remnants from the past that are emerging.

What a tremendous gift you give yourself and others by turning to face and meet them. You are allowing for the possibility that these energies and emotions can breathe—perhaps for the first time—and grow, change, modulate, and perhaps move on.

You are giving yourself and your body a gift, making space for new patterns to emerge.

But new patterns do not emerge because those yucky ones are gone, flushed out, and—thank goodness—pushed away. New patterns emerge from the energy of old patterns. They are given life from older patterns. The old wounding and the new healing are not two things. They are made of the same essence. In a way, they are always together.

☀

When we dare to see that our preferences for what we want to happen occur on the same level as what is actually happening, we surrender the imagined part of who we are. Through wholehearted intimacy with what is unfolding here, we recognize our unbreakable connection and identity with the presence that *is* here.

You are much more the author of new patterns when you approach life consciously. When you are willing to meet what is arising for you in this moment, whatever that may be.

There is a release of body and mind in being this way. When we approach the body reverently, with a willingness to really listen, we allow it to speak its memory, share what was once rejected, and perhaps modulate into a slightly different pattern.

This is an absolutely healing and purifying process.

It is an activity of love.

It is not so much about getting rid of the painful storehouses of hurt that we all harbor but finally, at long last, feeling safe enough to welcome and embrace what we felt we could not before.

We don't know what will come up.

We don't need to enjoy or like what arises.

We shouldn't even demand that we feel better afterward.

However, we should know that we have a sacred responsibility in a way that no one else could possibly have of tending to and caring for these fragile and wondrous bodies.

For our logical minds, this is a process of patience, compassion, and humility.

Once again, this is an expression of love.

It is amazing that in a certain depth of intimacy with these words we find they are pointing to a place where there is no problem, technique, or time for strategy, separation, or relationship between mind and body to arise. We find that these words are at one and the same time pointing to, and also part of, the immediacy of this moment. Part of this one life. It is as though each moment is calling us home to this.

six

medication

I remember being shamed by a sponsor in early recovery
when I shared I was going to a methadone clinic. This
person told me that I wasn't really clean. That my sobriety wasn't real. That I had just moved to a less destructive
addiction.

I felt devastated at the time. I had been going to two or
more AA meetings every day, seeing two therapists, and
fearfully hanging on by what seemed like the thinnest
threads of hope and sanity. I thought if I just stayed clean
and didn't use, it would all get better somehow.

I remember praying every morning that I could be open
to new ways of being in the world. I didn't know what I
was praying to. If anything, it felt as though I was praying
to the unseen source of the words that I had heard inside
myself the morning after Christmas. The words that had
spoken "You never need to use again." I had reverence for
the power behind those words.

In that moment of shame and doubt, I questioned myself. I wondered if everything I was doing was worthless. Whether I had simply tricked myself again.

By some grace, I intuited that this person was mistaken in their perception of me in that moment. I *was* clean, and everything I was doing, including going to the methadone clinic, was healing and helping me.

Although this person was likely expressing and holding on to their idea of hope in the same way that I was doing for myself, I think it is important to examine this common notion in recovery groups that taking medication to help alleviate physical and psychological difficulty related to addiction is somehow cheating, less than, not real, or an easy way out.

Ultimately, maybe we don't need to take medicine long-term. But maybe we do. Does whether this is the case or not form a basis for what matters most to us in our hearts?

I don't take medicine, and have not for many years. However, I did need to take medicine then. I know some friends who have taken medicine for many years. It helps them. They no longer use, or feel compelled to use, but they also don't feel moved to stop taking medicine. And they are strong, brave, loving, and inspiring individuals.

The insistence that being clean and healthy should look a certain way reduces us and our winding journeys of life and recovery to a black or white oversimplification.

Healing and wellness are processes. They are not end points. And they are certainly not prescribed end points reached when one has stopped taking medicine and not engaged in their addictive behavior of choice for a certain period of time.

Although it may feel like healing and wellness are distant goals at certain points in your recovery, you do yourself a favor if you give yourself permission to recognize that even in the midst of tremendous difficulty and craving, there is—as mindfulness meditation teacher Dr. Jon Kabat Zinn says—more right about who you are than wrong.

This wholesome truth is true even if you feel there is nothing but craving and suffering present. It is true even if healing feels like an end point that you can come one step closer to by just making it through the next hour. This is certainly a valuable perspective. However, along with it, can you also know that – in this moment – you are okay? Can you feel proud for who you are? Exactly as you are. Right in the midst of shame and self-disgust. And even as you continue to fight to feel better.

Some of us need help navigating the physical process of withdrawal and something to take the edge off of psychological craving.

To be able to heal, we need to feel. We don't need to re-traumatize or overwhelm ourselves for the sake of an ideal or image of what recovery should look like, and when that should happen. If we refuse to listen to ourselves and what we need, even if all we know is that we need help, we do ourselves a disservice.

This is not a call to continue using or to give in to each craving because it hurts less. These justifications are simply a more destructive version of the language used by "dry drunks," who, although no longer using, may often feel trapped in similar emotional and psychological patterns that ran their lives while actively using.

What if there was another way of being with addictive energy, where you don't lose yourself in or wall yourself off from the energy, but rather begin to explore and listen to it? Sometimes, to be able to listen to these very strong and frightening energies of addiction, you need help.

In certain cases medication can provide that help.

Medication may take the edge off your psychological and physical distress in such a way that you are actually able to start meeting and exploring the parts of yourself that you turned to drugs, alcohol, work, sex, food, technology, thought, or other people to cover up and numb in the first place. Giving yourself this space can be the most honest thing you can do. The alternative is retraumatization, taking on too much too soon—an understandable impulse when we are suffering under the weight of addiction—and ending up using again.

Or we find other ways to numb. We reshape our identity into some idea of what recovery looks like, paralyzed by fear, and wall ourselves off from facing what scares us most.

This doesn't really help either.

The house of fear constructed from recovery philosophies that uphold long-distance mental views of addiction, is less overtly damaging than the house of fear we lived within while we were actively using. However, it is a halfway house. More often than not, we remain trapped in a fearful house of recovery, stuck, and not really free.

Can you look inside and ask yourself what you need?

No one else can answer this question for you.

How can you begin to face the parts you have disowned in a way that you don't re-traumatize yourself?

How can you begin to lovingly be with these parts?

As you may have heard before, anything that has been kept in a cage for a long time may not be happy when you first encounter it. There may be screaming and agony. You may want to die. To shut the door. To numb out. This is expected and normal. Of course you don't want to feel pain.

Can the resistance you may feel in response to the presence of pain be just as lovingly allowed and accepted as the pain itself?

※

Can you allow the pain and the reactions you have about your pain to develop a relationship?

Can you allow both to enter the same room to finally spend some time with each other?

※

You are the mediator here, of course. You are the one choosing the depth of intimacy and the duration of these meetings. You are the witness, ground, and mother to your experience. You are the inner space where this most sacred meeting between pain and its resistance takes place.

When unseen, this meeting of pain and resistance creates the experience of a separate suffering me, desperately trying to keep a head above water in a hostile world.

When seen, this very same meeting of pain and resistance frees us and reminds us of what we really are.

The sacred meeting of pain and its resistance must be welcomed moment by moment.

☀

The fearful, strategizing mind creates an idea of what this meeting looks like, hoping to do it once and then retreat back to the caverns of fear from whence it came. But this does not seem to be the way life works.

Freedom is not a result of remaining in a place of comfortable conditioning, even though there may be a loud story that tells us that this is indeed the case. Freedom is realized through a willingness to meet what is arising. Whether it is painful or not, whether there is tension or not, is not so important.

☀

This recognition may change the felt experience of pain so that it is no longer the most compelling part of experience. In these moments, the felt sense of presence draws the attention more than any particular feeling of discomfort. In these moments, the heart quietly and simply loves and knows itself as always and already connected to the wholeness of this wondrous moment.

What is it like for you to welcome pain and its resistance right now . . . and now? Can you feel the visceral waves of pain and resistance ebb and flow as part of the perfectly natural movement of life that you are?

seven

learning to feel

We live in a culture that glorifies the intellect and is largely addicted to sensationalism. It is a culture that mistakes drama for feeling. That unconsciously preys upon our individual and collective fears and tries to package and sell the inherent wisdom of the already open and welcoming heart into imagined boxes of commoditized sensational catharsis.

That same culture unconsciously preys on our deep yearning to feel connected with ourselves, and our communities. It unconsciously manipulates our natural human need for connection, which we so often forget, and infuses it with a healthy dose of fear. It tells us we do not have what we need. It tells us that only if we work more, earn more, diet more, or learn more will we finally, at last, realize and satisfy our human need and birthright for connection and wholeness.

Most of the time we are culturally rewarded for dissociating from our bodies and feelings and placing all our attention on tasks that demand everything from us. In many cases, the extent to which we are successful at doing this impacts the extent to which we are rewarded in our jobs, economies, or social systems. Which keeps us trapped in this cycle.

It is important to recognize how challenging it can be to step outside of an addictive cycle and enter into a world where people largely do not discuss their feelings. To open our eyes to a world that has little vocabulary for basic psychological process. The pain you experienced as a sensitive person in this type of world may be one reason you headed down the path of addiction in the first place. To see if it was possible to numb the pain.

What if this pain was not an indication of brokenness but of inherent health?

It hurts to repress parts of ourselves. This is a healthy indication that something is out of balance. Just because there is an unspoken agreement from the collective to repress parts of who we are does not mean that it is healthy or that it reflects wisdom. In most social contexts, we are expected to put on a smile, talk about the weather, and pretend that we are not even really present. Of course this hurts! Even if we don't subscribe to this, it still hurts.

In recovery, it is possible to honor the challenging process of rebuilding relationships without numbing yourself from the natural, healthy pain you may frequently experience.

It may sometimes feel quite lonely. As you look around your new world with the fresh, grateful, and deconstructive eyes of someone who has survived the throes of addiction, who has danced closely for a while with darkness, you may notice everyone seems to be rushing around from one thing to another in a dream- like and ghost-like manner.

Collectively, there seems to be little questioning of the business-as-usual cultural prescription: Go to school, get a job, start a family, save for retirement, and die quietly.

Let me be clear. There is absolutely nothing wrong with the actual life events and choices that this cultural prescription points to. Each one of these life events and situations can be enriching, connecting, and life affirming.

However, when these activities are unquestioningly sub-scribed to as a recipe for happiness, we feel cut off from the creative, spontaneous, and beautiful wisdom of our human spirit. When we feel this, we feel unfulfilled. When we blindly experience not feeling full, most of us look for ways to fill up and not hurt so much.

We turn to the next item that can be acquired or crossed off the never-ending to-do list that has become our unexamined measuring stick for happiness. When we are unaware of being identified with culturally prescribed patterns of being, it is difficult to enjoy or appreciate the unique ways that we might start a family or how we may learn to creatively dance with the fluid and energetic interchange between world and self that we call work. This hurts. And it is unnecessary.

⁎

Learning to feel is perhaps one of the most important things we can do for ourselves in recovery. This might be better phrased as the process of becoming aware of, and trusting in, the feelings that are already here. Much of addiction is the result of an unseen fear of intimacy with emotion and sensation. As a result of this unseen fear, many of us turned to our substance or behavior of choice to numb out.

Now, entering into the world of the so called well-adjusted, we may hold hope that we have made it past the hard part and can now settle into our cultural armchairs. We may hope to feel better and be more functional by mimicking the lives of those we see around us.

Unfortunately, this has not been my experience. We can be sober, a well-functioning citizen, but still be miserable for everybody—including ourselves—to be around. Addiction arose for many of us because of deep wounding, but addiction also left deep wounds that cannot be numbed by the opium of collective agreement.

When we actually take a closer look at the lives of those we might hope to emulate, we find that they are riddled with less overt forms of addiction.

One of the many examples of this is the addiction to screens. There is nothing inherently wrong with screen time. Especially since the COVID-19 pandemic, technology allows us to connect with each other in ways that would otherwise be impossible. I work remotely at the moment and could not do so without access to screens. However, it is also so commonplace to see people who are completely addicted to their screens. It is heartbreaking to see someone glued to their screen while they are walking, eating, and sometimes even talking with other people standing in front of them. I know how this feels and it hurts. It is a commonplace and ingrained habit for many in the world today. I recently ate breakfast at a restaurant that offered free deserts to patrons who surrendered their phones to a basket while they ate. When I asked the hostess how they didn't go out of business, she smiled and said that they only gave away one or two deserts every week.

My friend, you are not alone. Not only are you not alone but others could learn from you and your journey with addiction. Your journey is not a wrong turn or detour leaving you desolate, beat up, and in last place in the race of life. Whatever that is. Although it can feel exactly like this when we behold our life situations in early recovery from the culturally prescribed values of what constitutes wealth, success, and abundance, it is absolutely not true.

How can we live in this world with others while holding a job, raising a family, and saving for retirement? This is a deep inquiry.

How can you be part of this collective but also feel deeply enough into yourself that you are first and foremost moved by your own wisdom? How can your inner promptings inform and motivate your actions rather than cripple them?

For myself, learning to feel is so important. It is not taught in schools or encouraged in many friendships or relationships and adults may not have modeled it well for us growing up. Psychotherapy can help us become consciously aware of our already well functioning capacity to feel. Similarly, meditation can help. Close relationships with others in which we can honestly and safely share how we are doing, learning to play an instrument, painting, journaling, and walking in nature can help so much.

How can we learn to befriend our emotions?

Even the most painful and overwhelming ones?

How can we begin to love ourselves in the midst of challenge?

The answers to these questions are not thoughts that the mind can take up as a perspective and then apply. The answers to these questions are living inquiries and involve the processes of both consciously dipping our toes into places of wounding and suffering inside and also following threads of inspiration, creativity, and joy in our lives.

☀

No one can do this for you.

We might begin by playing a sport or exercising more. Becoming more in touch with our body and sensations, and seeing that we can trust the body more than we normally think, can provide a sensational familiarity and language for us to start more intimately exploring our feelings. It is in the body that emotions can be worked with most directly.

☀

As the last rays of the setting sun cast wide mystic shadows, the sky painted in dimming oranges and reds, birds hushed, how do you find yourself? In these moments, you are likely lost in feeling. Which doesn't need to be explosive or cathartic. The love in these moments is subtler—a soft appreciation and connection with what is that is felt in the body—particularly the heart.

The mind doesn't need to confirm and say "Yes, that's true" for this knowing to emerge. It might, but if you are honest, don't you just feel it? Isn't the mental commentary secondary? If you are honest, aren't you already living in intimate connection with your feelings, communities, and environments? Isn't the connection you most yearn for already present?

This intuitively felt connection with the wholeness of life may or may not always feel pleasant. It may also not always look like the noisy, fitful, cathartic image of connection that we often see in movies or hear on the radio. We often mistake emotion with feeling. Emotion is largely the sensational counterpart to mental belief. If the tip of the belief, "I am no good" is experienced as a clenching thought in the head, the base of that belief is experienced as sensational clenching in the body.

When we unhook from being totally enamored with the mental spray of the mind and the sensational vortexes of emotion it spins—which are often showy, dramatic, fast, and what we have been told feeling and connection look like—can we discover for ourselves what connection actually feels like in this moment . . . and again in this one?

Can we let ourselves feel and be moved by the ocean of connection that is the basis of this moment?

eight

identification
with thought

Sometime during the first year of sobriety, I remember walking through a McDonald's parking lot on a hot summer day. The blacktop was scorching, and I was sweating profusely, feeling miserable about my life. In the midst of the discomfort, a very strong urge to use arose. I felt totally blindsided and confused. I remember shamefully thinking that I had done something wrong. It felt like the other shoe had finally dropped. The urge was so strong that there was not a sense that it was objectively happening to me. There was just craving and mental agony. It felt like I had already relapsed. Somehow in the middle of this, I remembered that I had been told to call my sponsor if something like this happened. Luckily I did. After we talked for a bit, the urge lessened a little. I still felt miserable but I wasn't as deeply in the woods as I had been before the call.

He said something during that conversation that has stuck with me and which is so important to look into. He said, "If we relapsed every time we had a thought of using, nobody would be clean or sober."

When we allow our entire sense of who we are to be dictated and directed by the thoughts in our minds, we limit ourselves. When we can only hear the voice of the judging mind, who appears as a "me" that chastises our "good" or "bad" thoughts, we limit ourselves.

As we become aware that the judge and the judged are both thought forms that we are aware of, we may feel that we are discovering a great truth. We may feel that we are more the dynamic power of knowing awareness—aware— than a fixed and static "me" at the center of it all who knows what is right and wrong. We may feel the release of not being pushed around by the contents of our minds. We may notice that it has always been this way.

However, most of us also quickly find out how strong the momentum of our habituated resistive relationship to life is and how often it asserts itself. It is quite natural for this to happen. However, if resistance appears unconsciously in the midst of seeing the rest of the contents of our minds as inseparable from the awareness knowing them, this living wisdom is remarkably spun into a new identity based on being a no one who knows! In these moments, we feel comfortably numb and a little distant from the rest of life. There is no end to the number of ways we can weave identity.

Now that we've identified the fluid nature of thinking and identification with thinking, and how difficult it is to pin down exactly who or what we are, let's explore this process a little more.

Let's consider an example. When we try to repress or shut out thoughts, or when we identify with and become identical with a particular point of view, we feel powerless beneath the energy of that thought pattern.

Isn't this curious?

How is it that we can seemingly become controlled by a thought pattern? Who is this "me" that opposes or supports a certain movement of thought? Can you find them? What do they look like?

Are your answers to these questions also thoughts that belong to that same "me"?

What if your resistance and attachment to particular thoughts were seen as part of that same thought stream?

What would remain of the sense of a separate "me" when identity is divested of its resistive and craving-fueled perspectives?

Can we look again?

Can you see that resistance and attachment are known in exactly the same way as the thoughts that are being resisted or craved? As a byproduct of this seeing, it is also revealed that because you are aware of resistance, resistance cannot be fundamentally who you are. What then is left? Who are you when your seeing not only includes contents of the mind but also the subtle pushes and pulls toward or away from those contents?

☀

In this seeing, which sees resistance to a thought as well as the thought itself equally, is there anything in particular you can point to and say "There I am."?

"There I am" is another thought.

Is there a clenching? A resistance to this inquiry that might say, if it could speak, "Stop this. What are you talking about? Isn't it obvious I'm right here?"

This too is known and seen in exactly the same way as the thought "Here I am." Therefore, this clenching cannot be who you are fundamentally.

Is there anything to take control over or direct you when you see from this place? Doesn't this open space of seeing include all urges and resistance to urges? Doesn't it include all thoughts and counter-thoughts?

Sure, the tension and unpleasant sensation of competing thoughts may be felt, but when there is an awareness of this self-perpetuating pattern of resistance and what is resisted, there is also freedom. It is seen in these moments that all of it is somehow miraculously occurring within you—within the space and presence of this very moment. Even if it is stormy, cloudy, and very unpleasant. Even if your nervous system is on edge, and you feel unsafe. Even if your body and mind are clenching and you notice the beginnings of dissociation. This is all your space. All of this is occurring within you. These sensations, feelings, and thoughts could not possibly be fundamentally who you are. This is not a call to nihilism. It is not a call to identify with a new thought pattern that says "There is no one here," or "I am presence." Thoughts like these also belong to this same inner landscape. The point is that these contents of consciousness depend on you, not the other way around. You could never be known as a content of the mind or the body.

Isn't it curious that you are always here and now? Could you conceive of a time other than now when you are? Or a place other than here where you are? Although you can certainly have thoughts about yourself and your history, aren't they always experienced right here? The word *here* does not reference a location in space, and the word *now* does not reference a moment in time. Here and now point toward the very ordinary presence from which these words emerged and out of which they are now rolling off the page and being read. It is as though each thought is borrowing existence from you to exist at all.

You are the knowing, alive, present, buzzing space in which all inner and outer life unfolds, which is not captured by these words. These words are simply momentary carriers of that presence. Meaningful and alive right now. Now, gone. Just like everything else.

Isn't it curious that thoughts about the past happen here in this moment, in the same way as thoughts about the future? They both happen within you, within this moment, even though they can produce the appearance of originating from another place and moment and the very persistent sensation that reports that you are somehow tied to or dependent on them.

Isn't the seeing of this itself freeing? Not needing to correct or necessarily do anything with the thoughts but simply to see them as thoughts. This seeing offers the opportunity that freedom from addiction is not to be won down the road when you no longer have urges or cravings. It reveals freedom as something to be discovered here, lovingly, in the midst of urges and cravings.

Can you become interested in the experience of craving and your reactions to this universal and inherited pattern of wanting?

What is it like to be so intimate with it that there is no mental space between you and what has been labeled craving?

When you are consciously close to craving, it is no longer a concept that is feared or hated from a point in the middle forehead where "me" also seems to be located. In these moments, craving is very simply and directly experienced from within the sensation itself. At the heart of craving, you do not find the rigid solidity that is anticipated from a long-distance, fearful, mental view of it but rather a spacious and freeing felt presence. By working intimately with craving, you discover a deeper dimension to who you are. A dimension that is naturally resilient and already at peace with what is unfolding within it. You might say that this dimension emerges from the heart of this moment as a point of potential, while also somehow embracing the entirety of the world in its being.

☼

Can you see how often your actions are continuations of your thoughts, constituted by your understanding of who you are and your relationship with the thoughts, emotions, and sensations within you?

How would you act and how would you feel inside if you felt pushed around less by the contents of your mind and body? This is not something to be done or achieved. Being pushed around less is an immediate and direct response to simply seeing something as it is.

Again and again.

This is not a suggestion that you should do nothing. Doing nothing is just a "negative" mental identification with the movement of life.

Freedom from being pushed around is a byproduct of seeing yourself the way you really are. This means freedom is not dependent on any situation, and it does not require the absence of craving or difficulty. Freedom is to be found in the midst of all situations, events, cravings, and difficulties. This is the only place freedom could ever possibly be known. Through clear seeing of your experience. This one.

Take heart that this is not as black and white as thought would make it seem. There is a spectrum of how aware we are of the ways that we apparently formulate rigidly separate and painful identities for ourselves through unconsciously resisting some aspect of what is. And take heart that each moment is wildly new. Sure, there is memory. There is certainly a momentum to the habits of the body and of the mind. But though these energetic patterns may appear very strongly, they appear anew, right here and now.

Eventually, the pain of resisting what is seems to bring us to the revelation that we are already perfectly held, welcomed, and accepted here. Just as everything else. And that who we are is harder to pin down than we used to think.

Herein lies one of the gifts of addiction.

The tremendous physical and psychological pain involved in craving and resisting craving and in gradually developing intimacy with these strong, roiling, almost unbearable patterns of mind and body offers you a rare opportunity to discover a new way of being.

Often, there is simply no other option. Life opens its eyes to another way. The subtle unseen clenching and pushing—the energetic response of rejecting this moment in some way—that underlies the sense of being a separate person struggling underneath the weight of tremendous inner and outer pressures simply can no longer be endured. Consciousness opens its eyes, and recognizes that there is an aspect of itself—its essence—that is already free from the limitations and pains of life experience.

Possibly just for a moment.

There is perhaps a noticing that right now words are being read and that these words—these ones—don't really reference or touch anything except themselves. Right now there is just this. We could call it reading, but that is a label. Which is as fine a label as any to use but I want to make sure that we understand each other. The wonder in simply reading these words right now is so new, and the mental habit patterns stirred in the wake of hearing a familiar word can feel anything but. The compulsion to label and mentally understand what is happening can often emerge from a natural but also unconscious and fearful resistance to the largeness of this moment. When unseen, this resistance can create the sensation of a separate struggling me who has no time to lose and who needs to figure it all out. Who needs labels to categorize and make sense of this unsafe moment that it finds itself in.

The revealed wisdom of addiction is wrapped into each moment through the very fact of its being. Each and every moment is of the same essential nature. The most blissful and pleasant moments are of essentially the same nature as the most painful moments of self-entrenched struggling and craving.

Once again, you are invited to look inward and see if you can become interested in thinking colored by craving. As you read right now, craving may subtly appear as labeling, wanting, or as the need to understand. Most of us, most of the time, will experience some degree of craving when we check in. This is not a problem.

As you check in, can you notice the sensational qualities, shapes, and movements of these thoughts? This question is not designed to change or get rid of craving laden thinking. It is less about what to do with the content at first, or whether it is right or wrong, and more about seeing and honestly welcoming it. When we fully meet and welcome craving, it reveals something quite amazing and very freeing. Intimacy with craving reveals it to be a natural movement of life, fluidly connected with the rest of life.

What is revealed is that the contents of this moment are in fact contents. Contents that are changing. And which could not ever really constitute or describe who you are.

This revelation arises through the aliveness of this moment. It can't be formulated, packaged, and carried with you outside of the body into a realm of transcendent witnessing or watching where nothing really touches or impacts you. These conceptual strategies are something that thought understandably tries to do with revelation—out of fear. As we oscillate back and forth and in and out of this seeing of content and ourselves the way we are, it is natural to wish the peace of this revelation to always be clearly felt and experienced in body and mind.

Through this wish, you may notice yourself trying to grab hold of past moments of clarity and apply them to this moment to escape feeling painful sensations of craving or other difficulty. However, when you pause and reassess, you find that this strategy doesn't pan out. Each moment is totally new. And each moment carries within it the revelation of who we are. Try as we might, it seems that we can never really carry the revelation of a previous moment with us into this one.

When you feel overwhelmed and unconsciously tell yourself that it is not okay to feel this way—which we all do, over and over again—and either identify with or shun your experience out of fear, know that this is fodder for the next moment. These energies of identification, addiction, pain, and challenge will emerge again—slightly differently—and the opportunity will arise anew to notice and see.

Let us see if we can stop beating ourselves up and shaming ourselves for not being perfect. For not somehow figuring it all out on the first try. Or the one thousandth try.

What is it like to become more interested in the particular nature of this moment than in our track records of how well or poorly we are doing? Whether we are understanding or not.

Can you begin to open to a wonder that is more interested and in love with this moment than in any story you have about it?

nine

creativity

What is creativity? Is it something we do? Is it something done to us? Are we naturally creative? Is it something that we can develop or evoke? Why would we want to?

Often the mind associates creativity with an art form. It says something like "Oh, you're a musician. You must be creative." And generally considers work such as keeping track of finances or filing taxes as dry or boring.

Is it true?

Is creativity identical with art or science? Does it belong to any discipline, practice, or thing?

What if the creative disciplines and art forms are simply agreed upon collective containers that more easily allow or help us recognize creative expression when it arises? I've listened to some very dry music that was technically perfect but which lacked any spark, and I have watched in amazement as the process of financial planning on an Excel spreadsheet took on a life of its own.

What is creative expression?

If we look closely, we can see it at work in each and every moment.

This moment arises from a creative wellspring.

When we talk of creativity, do we limit it to an expression of life that seems to originate from and be contained within the body?

The body is just a small part of life.

If you listen closely, you can hear symphonies playing out in the morning woods. You can see canvases of colors and shapes being masterfully crafted before your eyes in each moment—finished just as soon as they dissolve and modulating into new, equally beautiful masterpieces in the next moment. Life is always creating. Isn't this what we really mean when we talk about creativity?

Moreover, aren't we all so perfectly creative to begin with? This beautiful murmuring heart and gentle breath call forth different songs and dances in each and every moment. Life is creating right now, in this very moment, a unique and wondrous world within you. Sensations that you have never felt before in exactly the same way. Thoughts that from one perspective may appear stale and old but which from another are taking unique trajectories through the apparent sensational center and origin of self in the brain. That simply pop up and disappear. Not unlike lightning bugs in the summer. How absolutely amazing! There are symphonies playing out within us all the time! Did you call for these thoughts? These sensations? These feelings? Did you know what would happen to you today? Don't your responses to these questions arise just as mysteriously as everything else? Even sensations of clenching and fear.

Yes, there is memory. But isn't it always Memory! When we look closely, memory is discovered to be beautiful, fresh, and unique.

☀

Researchers have estimated that we have around seventy thousand thoughts each day. This works out to something like one to two thoughts every second. Further, some United States researchers estimate that approximately ninety percent of these are repeats, and more than half of them tend toward negativity in some way. From this perspective, we are essentially living in thought-created prisons for most of the day.

This paints a pretty dreary picture of our inner lives. Many of us will nod in agreement—at one time or another we have all felt inundated by the repetitive, compulsive, negative aspects of our patterns of thinking.

When we are not aware of the ever-fleeting nature of our thoughts, we are also unaware that they are behaving exactly as they should and that they perfectly belong here. In these moments, we are also unaware that these thoughts have arisen before we even have had time to arise ourselves to pass judgment on them. We feel as though we are the orchestrator of it all—an "I" behind the eyes—solid, separate, and at the center of it all. What responsibility! When this is the case, it is hard to see that our reactionary like-dislike relationship with the contents of our minds does not actually make us any more safe, secure, or happy. In moments such as these, it absolutely does seem true that we need to fight to feel okay. It does appear that we are trapped within the stale confines of oppressive, perhaps critical and negative, mental worldviews.

However, this kind of thinking does not necessarily need to be limiting. Although the time-bound, thinking mind can indeed be limiting, it is closely tied to memory – and memory in and of itself is a beautiful aspect of perception.

From one perspective, memory does not detract from our experience of the directness of this moment. Rather, memory acts as a structure upon which more elaborate patterns can evolve and be directly experienced.

Take the memory required to play a piece of music on the piano. This is a tremendous effort, and it is hard to scratch the surface of a Beethoven piano sonata, for instance, if one has not memorized the finger positions, and understood the larger patterns present in the score.

Memory allows us to construct and open into deeper and exquisitely satisfying aspects of human experience. The interesting thing about music is that these so called "preliminary" exercises or "practices" of memorizing are not stale if they are approached creatively. From a certain perspective, there is never memory. There is just this. Even breaking down a score into small sections with the aim of eventually incorporating them into the larger piece of which they are a part is fresh and creative. When we notice this, then the time spent breaking the score into palatable chunks is not experienced as drudgery leading up to some imagined end point.

In fact, only when we are breaking down a score into palatable chunks do we actually feel the freedom we usually imagine lies in wait at the end of a long journey of learning and effort. These more 'ordinary' moments along the way then don't feel as if they are just propping up, or rotting, underneath whatever it is that we are waiting to hear during the so called "final performance." A piece of music is never played the same way twice. And yet, it could never be played at all without lots and lots of memory.

Although memory, in and of itself, does not lead us to feel that we are trapped within the confines of thought-created prisons, there are structures of thought that do obscure the sense of ever-fresh creativity. This is true when there is resistance—or clenching—behind thought that is not seen.

When this clenching is unseen, it remains unconscious, and then its uniqueness and vitality as an ever-moving and changing focal point within awareness appears as the origin of awareness—the center me—that has had the same thought thousands of times. Which is now fixed, right here, and taking a stand against this or that.

Isn't this all just another story—including this inquiry and discussion right here?

The story says it has understood what it is doing and that it doesn't need to look again. That, since it has understood the way it is, it can then create a label to apply to other moments, to help simplify and contain the unknown. This is a story largely motivated by the fear of change and the fear of danger. It is a viscerally learned and addictive resistance to what is that has played an important role in survival and evolution for many years.

With this is mind, can we reexamine what we mean when we say that something is creative? Can we see that life is naturally creative and that, as a part of life, we also are creative?

Life is not separate from this moment. The joy felt in creating is so often the joy of feeling connected with something larger than ourselves. It is the natural joy felt in the wake of not being unconsciously driven by resistance to what is happening here. The joy of allowing ourselves to relax and trust the ever-winding movements and expressions of life within us. In these moments, we feel more connected to ourselves, to others, and to life as a whole.

One of the gifts of addiction is that it teaches us in a very painful way what resisting and trying to numb out parts of life that we find unacceptable does to us. The visceral story that addiction told was that we would not be fulfilled unless we numbed through our behavior of choice. This story was itself rooted in the belief that it was not okay to feel the sensations, thoughts, or emotions within us. The entire world was reduced to a very linear and one-dimensional story line about what was okay and what was not okay, what was worthy of attention and what was not, what gives happiness and what doesn't.

The unseen resistance to what is, which obscures the felt connection and joy of creativity, is so large and present in addiction that in honestly working with it, we can't help but get insight into how numbing what we don't like—whether we do it through addictive behaviors or mental stories—impacts happiness. We ultimately discover that unconscious resistance limits us to narrow ideas and story lines, cut off from the feeling of aliveness and connection inherent in every moment.

Let me be clear: This has nothing to do with getting rid of stories or throwing it all out the window and living recklessly. In our own ways, most of us have tried that already. This is more about noticing that with the simplest changing of focal point, almost like a camera lens adjusting focus, we can open out and see that the doer, the one who is apparently driving the whole show and trying to arrange a set of life circumstances that is agreeable, is itself a result of unseen clenching. Not unlike the unseen, clenching resistance driving so much of addiction.

Through this seeing, in the midst of memory, structure, rules, and culture, we discover freedom. We see that although we live in a structured and conditioned world, we are inherently free of the limitations of these structures. Moreover, we find in these structures the ingredients for fresh expression and connection. We see aliveness and vitality in the structures themselves.

Isn't this beautiful? In the very simplest change of focus, we free ourselves. We don't need to go anywhere or do anything or even get rid of our most painful habits. We simply need to see them as they are. As habits.

In this seeing, right in this moment, you free yourself. You can't take this seeing-being with you to the next moment, or bank it for later. It is always right now that you are free. This can be scary to your mental constructs—to your beliefs about what you need to be free. A fearful story may arise that interprets the invitation to change focus as a command to give up the structures—job, family, home, money—you have been working so hard to secure to finally feel okay. This story may say that it is lunacy—unsafe, dangerous—and that it will all fall apart if you were to do it.

Let me assure you that you don't need to throw any of the structures out. Really. That would just be replacing one structure with another—the structure of "no structure." What is being invited is more of a seeing and way of being than something that you do. Nothing is really gained through being with life in this way. It has always been like this. There has simply been a lot of fog in there. Which is very natural. Fog is part of life. And, fog burns off in the sunlight.

Freedom is simply a matter of seeing. Not by the one who may now be trying to see but through an aliveness—a being-seeing that simply and directly knows, right now, that even though there may be tension, resistance, struggle, and clenching, all of this is happening. Everything is welcome in this space that holds the one who doesn't feel safe—and not from a mile-high detached state of witnessing but as the loving, supportive, aware space that supports and permeates everything.

Yes, feeling unsafe feels bad. No arguing with that.

However, what if peace was larger than feeling good or bad?

What if there was a peace within the sense of badness?

What if within the feeling of being bad there was a dancing, pulsating heartbeat of life?

In allowing this, your nervous system may relax a little bit.
Perhaps you feel a bit better, even though nothing really
seems to have changed.

What is this aliveness that is still here now? How interesting that unconsciously resisting this moment can create the
experience of being a separate and divided person—both
inside and out. Have you noticed that you argue with more
than just people in your life? If we are honest, most of us
will find that we argue and are in disagreement with ourselves much of the time.

This splitting off also happens when it is foggy outside.
When you are walking through dense fog, there are only
small pockets of clarity. You may feel a little uneasy, that
you are strenuously focusing to discern landmarks around
you to know where you are.

In foggy moments, you have a sense only of what is right
in front of you and can't see the larger context. This can be
scary. It can feel as though you are not safe, and need to be
on guard.

However, if we see our psychological journeys through
fog as natural and expected life experiences, the situation opens up a bit. When we allow ourselves to viscerally
experience feeling foggy or confused and don't take refuge
in the hologram-like mental worlds of seeking, strategizing, and safety that are spun out of resisting the visceral

experience of confusion, the fog may remain, but a part of us clearly knows that fog, muddledness, and confusion are not really limiting. How could they be? They are patterns, like any others. Patterns of fogginess arise, and if unseen resistance arises in their wake, then we also appear to arise as a separate "I" searching for safety. The sense of separateness is a natural result of the pristine expression of fog, and our resistance to it. These patterns are here, and so often give birth to the feeling of being a limited and separate person. They are also here even before we can try to turn this observation into a strategy to feel better, to welcome or accept the fog in order to do the "right" thing—perhaps hoping it will go away if we are "good."

In this awareness, can we experiment with relaxing into a visceral intimacy with confusion or fogginess as it arises? Eventually, when sunshine burns fog off of water, it is seen that there was never anything separate from anything else. There was just the totality of the moment—including water, sunshine, and patches of fog.

In these moments, instead of the nature of fog, we feel ourselves to be of the nature of light. However, aren't both light and fog known? Aren't they both felt—one as an open, embodied heartfulness, the other as a clenching, fearful, headfulness? One reflects life as it is in clear seeing of the way things are. The other does not. However, aren't they both aspects of this one life? Light feels much more connected to life, while fogginess does not. But can disconnection—which hurts so much—also be okay? We are embodied after all. Can the viscerally felt sense of disconnection or separateness be welcomed and itself revealed as a thread of connection? Is it possible? This is a deep inquiry.

Let us become interested in our experience. Let us open to the wonder of it all. Are these thoughts even yours? Don't they just pop in and out of existence so mysteriously? It is breathtaking and a homecoming when we slow down enough to be with this process of life combustion that is continuously birthing never before seen worlds of the most vivid creation.

How amazing!

How creative!

ten

therapy

Therapy can be helpful, inspired, healing, or dry. Sometimes it can even be harmful.

A large part depends on your intentions. Are you just going through the motions? Are you telling the therapist what you think they want to hear? Or what your partner, family, friends, or court want the therapist to hear? Are you using the therapist to corroborate bitterness? To avoid really being honest with yourself about how you are feeling? To get someone off your back?

There are well-intentioned therapists who will consciously or unconsciously do these things for us—who will listen to us no matter what we say and nod, smile, and agree.

And this can be healing.

Don't get me wrong. To a certain extent, having someone just listen to whatever we say, without judging, putting up a fight, getting angry, or doing much of anything at all can be helpful.

So often we have not been able to express ourselves safely. The ability to express even unhealthy behavioral or psychological patterns without being chastised—even if we are not exploring these patterns, are unaware there are other ways of responding, or are hurting ourselves with our behavior—is to an extent healing.

However, when we feel unsafe expressing ourselves, we may continue the same unhealthy behavior but without much sense of connection or support from others. We remain blind to the pattern and to ourselves, and we feel isolated and alone. We are hurt twice.

When someone really hears us, even if they have vacated the room to do so—leaving only an empty mirror in their place—we feel a sense of acceptance that can be healing. We hurt ourselves only once.

When we feel we can't take ownership of a destructive behavioral or emotional pattern, we rely on other people or life experience to help us. If no one is there, the process of learning and growing is generally much slower. When we don't have someone to reflect our blind spots, we usually keep doing the same thing.

However, the therapeutic relationship can be so much more than talking to a reflective, supportive person. It can help us not only to feel that we are seen and accepted—even in our destructive behavior—but also to grow and heal more directly. So many of our wounds are relationship-based to begin with.

We do ourselves a favor by finding a therapist who doesn't leave the room when we sit together in session.

We do ourselves a favor by finding a therapist who offers us not just a mirror, but also the inescapable human dynamic involved in authentic human relationship.

Who appropriately shares their felt experience of sitting in the room with us.

Who knows that no one grows, hurts, or heals alone.

It is a collaborative process, and the relationship is so important.

Therapy can help us develop inner tools to work with challenging emotions and destructive thought patterns.

That sounds like a textbook answer, but the actual process is anything but predictable. It is usually messy. At times it can be very painful, and we may wonder why we are doing it at all. This makes perfect sense. Of course it hurts to look inside and see places where we are wounded.

This is why many people are not drawn to work with their psyche and do not have much familiarity with their inner life. Most of our energy goes into navigating our outer-life situations. We simply take for granted that the thoughts, feelings, and sensations that are experienced are given. They are who we are. What else is there to know?

Most of us have quite an identity investment in keeping up appearances. This is true not only to others but to ourselves as well. If you are a successful professional with a relatively functional family and a place to call home, and you have carved out a lifestyle that fits in well with collective ideas of success, you may not feel much motivation to look more deeply inside.

And yet for most people, there still seems to be something missing—albeit attributed to external factors. "If only there were a bigger home, a bonus that could pay for that vacation, life would be good."

More subtly, even if we have explored our inner selves, we often still fall into collective traps of how we should be—relying on spiritual or psychological frameworks for telling us whether or not we are understanding ourselves in the "right way." For instance, we can spend years policing our inner lives with spiritual concepts. We may fill our heads with platitudes such as "There is only love," "There is no one here," or "Accept what is" to such a degree that we forget what these phrases are actually pointing to. Through these sorts of practices we numb out and lose ourselves in an intellectual mantra that disconnects us even further from ourselves, our relationships with others, and our present moment experience.

Or we can strive to cram the dynamic, alive, psychic energy within us into reductive frameworks—labeling unique movements of life energy within us as remnants from our parents or of this or that period of our lives. Although it is so important to understand our history and to have a personal narrative that we find empowering and life-affirming, it is also so easy to pathologize this process and turn it into a way to avoid being intimate with the movement of life inside that these stories about our experience may be pointing to.

There is no end to the stories we can conjure for why an experience happened the way it did, or for why we may have rejected or resisted it. At a point, these narratives tend to reinforce our suffering, rather than help us become more intimate with it.

This doesn't mean we have to push stories aside in the process of healing. New or forgotten stories naturally emerge, modulate, leave, and then perhaps appear again in slightly different ways. This healing process is less about what we are uncovering and more about how honestly we are meeting, and not slamming the door at the first sign of discomfort.

Herein lies another gift of addiction. By amplifying dysfunctional behavioral patterns and beliefs to such a degree that we end up in treatment centers or courts, we often receive the unwanted gift of having no other option than to honestly see what is happening. It just hurts too much not to. After attempting to turn away from it for so long, addiction brings us to the revelation that there is no escape. This is a gift. It hurts, but it is a gift.

A good therapeutic relationship is a sacred space to receive this gift and explore oneself. Not because you are messed up or broken but because you are precious. This human life is a privilege, and so often we walk through it with blinders on, without a clue as to what is motivating our actions, influencing our feelings, or driving our thinking. Therapy can help us get in touch with ourselves and the unique currents of life running through us.

eleven

addiction and trauma

For many of us, intimacy with addiction also means intimacy with trauma. Although there are many definitions of trauma, here it refers to the natural, automatic, hard-wired, psychosomatic response to an overwhelming experience.

When we feel unsafe, our minds and bodies flip a switch and rev up hardwired programs to help us stay alive and cope with overwhelming sensation or impending harm.

This process is natural. Beautiful. And has saved our lives more than once. We should feel gratitude for the intelligence and wisdom of traumatic energy.

Clinical psychologist and trauma researcher Dr. Peter Levine speaks beautifully in his books about these hardwired strategies that we inherited from our animal ancestors. We owe much to the intelligence that arises to help protect us when our logical minds, with their complex magnificent ability to strategize, are out of answers or without the luxury to reason.

I remember the second time I nearly drowned. I had been whitewater canoeing and my boat flipped over in shallow water. I was stuck upside down and couldn't move my hands to pull the neoprene spray skirt designed to keep me in the boat and water out of the boat. After about 45 seconds of panicking underwater, the logical mind gave up. I felt defeated and ashamed. I surrendered myself to drowning and consciousness assumed a dissociated witness perspective, mostly vacating the body. A few seconds after this, my hands surprisingly mobilized themselves and began to pull and claw across the riverbed to reach deeper water. Once there, they ejected my body from the boat and I emerged gasping for air—amazed to be alive.

The intelligence in our bodies is tremendous. The intelligence that beats the heart and draws breath in every single moment is also present in overwhelming and traumatic experiences. It can be trusted and relied on, and it is very powerful and capable. It is the energy that allows a gazelle to evade a cheetah at speeds of up to 60 mph through quickly changing direction.

Imagine this energy. Imagine yourself in a life-or-death situation where your logical mind is short-circuited and thousands of years of finely tuned natural brilliance are coursing through your veins. You would move at lightning speed. And if you couldn't fight your way out or run away, this same energy would dislodge even the most deeply rooted visceral patterns of egocentric belief. By dissociating from the visceral clenching in the head that most of us take to be who we are—the "I" behind the eyes—the pain of attack or dying is lessened. From a dissociated perspective, the pain is not felt as personally or acutely. How amazing!

Now, imagine that this energy is interrupted, like interrupting a sneeze on steroids. When you feel a sneeze coming, with its energy building inside of you, and someone startles you, it feels awful. Afterward, you find that the energy of the sneeze is still there but not readily accessible anymore. It is stuck between the past and the present.

This is what happens for many people who have experienced traumatic events. It doesn't have to take a near-death experience for undischarged energy to be disruptive. We are so sensitive. Even the tiniest amount of undischarged overwhelm in our systems can create the sense of not really being here. It can lead to intolerable inner sensations and the sense of not being alright or safe. It can cause fear. Often we feel unsafe, but our logical minds don't have a sense of why, or where to look. Maybe trauma happened years ago. Maybe it is not remembered anymore. Maybe there is not the space, time, or sense of safety to cultivate an intimacy with these energies.

This is so natural. The fear responses of the logical mind that tries to understand, corral, and make these energies change, lessen, or go away are what it has evolved for. The logical mind is doing its job of trying to help the organism settle into an easier, safer, and more comfortable life.

It really is.

The organism wants to be at rest and feel peace. The primal, self-organized, visceral processes of trauma are also doing their part to achieve this. Traumatic intelligence is still fighting, revving up, and trying to rally all of the energies of this mind-body organism to ward off danger. Traumatic intelligence is lovingly trying to help you survive.

Is the energy and intelligence of trauma any different than the energy or intelligence of the thinking mind? Or the already open loving heart? Or the spacious vitality of the gut?

☼

Can you relax around which expression of life energy is right? Can you stop judging yourself for feeling overwhelmed or unsafe? Or for trying to feel safe? Can you see that your shaming and judging are perfectly understandable (though perhaps unskillful) strategies of the mind to deal with painful or overwhelming sensation, but that you ultimately need to do more than just take one side or the other?

You can remind your body of where you are and when you are. With your logical mind, you can help your body to understand that you are safe today. That you are safe right now. That it is safe to gently explore these energies of trauma. You can learn to feel from these energies rather

than from the stories the mind weaves around them, allowing the stories of the mind to be more like spray tumbling
off the tips of roiling sensational waves than some truth
about The Way It Is.

☀

Through this process of cultivating intimacy with traumatic energy, you can release patterns that no longer seem
relevant. You free these energies from their role of forming
your identity, even if the identity was painful, disliked,
or hated. You can become softly interested in what the
body would desire in this moment if it were free to move
about without traumatic patterning. What new currents
would surface?

Through this process, you can begin letting go—as an
expression of gratitude rather than a tactic or strategy—of
outdated energies that disconnect you from yourself or
your current surroundings. Letting go through deep feeling
and seeing. Letting go out of an interest in this body, here
and now, and this world, here and now. Letting go through
an intimate connection with this moment, not as a strategy
to make the energies go away—but trusting that you can
heal, and that life is leading the way. When you are intimate with life in this way, traumatic energy may seem less
of a "thing" that you can point to and more of a present
moment sensation within. Images may spin out. The body
may jerk or shake and feel temperature changes. There may
be roaring noises as sensation floods through the body.

Although these experiences can be intense, when we are intimately present to them, they are not problems, and they do not consume or define the presence that we are.

So much of addiction is turning away from overwhelming sensation. This is the same conditioned response of the mind to trauma. So, when we work with addiction, let us also learn to work with trauma. Perhaps much of our addiction was numbing ourselves to overwhelming emotions or sensations that the mind could not effectively push out of consciousness. Perhaps it was a way of coping with trauma.

Maybe we did not have the tools then to gradually begin to feel and experience these energies in ourselves.

But fortunately these energies are not there to hurt you. They are not present to make you feel miserable. You are not being punished.

These energies are a testament to your natural intelligence.

These energies are like raging whitewater rapids coursing through a narrow creek bed. Your nervous system is that creek bed. The force created by traumatic energy puts tremendous pressure on the nervous system and body. The ability of our bodies to rev into high gear and respond to threat, danger, and overwhelm in such a profound way protects and saves us when we are otherwise out of options.

As we find ourselves today, can we dare to explore these rapids and the roaring sound of water— overwhelm— which has haunted many of us for as long as we could remember. By turning towards the noise and seeing what it is actually pointing to, we may find that it is not as devastating and hopeless as we feared.

You may see that the water is still coursing around a huge boulder, dislodged by a past accident, in the middle of the stream. You may find that the crank of the dam upstream is wide open and there does not need to be as much energy present right now. Through present seeing of your inner and outer experience of sensational pressure, tuned in to but not swamped by how you imagine it to be right now, or how you would try to remember it to protect yourself, can you experience this sensational energy anew? You can let yourself be more intimate with strong sensation than the mind thinks safe, or the body remembers possible.

What would it be like? What new patterns of energy would be mobilized through this seeing? How would the intelligence of your body express itself? By turning toward the energies holding traumatic patterning, you give life new material with which to build, evolve, and grow.

You can trust that the ever-present intelligence of life— which you do not need to go looking for—will respond perfectly, as it is supposed to, through this seeing. You don't even need to do anything to free yourself.

It is that simple.

You simply need to see. To not only become aware of life on the level of form but to notice also the essential presence birthing form. To notice you *are* aware.

Through this seeing, you may find your hands moving to claw yourself across a creek bed, move a boulder out of it, or turn the crank of a dam upstream. And strangely, in these moments, these hands are not only your hands. It is life moving itself.

How amazing! You don't dissolve in trauma as your mind may have feared. You become the mover of trauma. You discover that traumatic energies are expressions of who you are. They are reclaimed and then serve to enrich this moment. Traumatic energy is not reclaimed by shoving it into a conceptual box, but by opening up and diving in. It is reclaimed when you allow a part of who you are to see itself as an essential energetic movement – and not just some glib idea of trauma.

From here, you may find that you no longer fear or wish these energies to be otherwise. Although there is always a part that resists the painful view of traumatic energy, you also gradually begin to understand that this view is habitual. That what you are actually seeing is life. And that when you dive in, you feel a satisfaction in being present to the sensational unraveling of the dance of traumatic energy within you. In that inner weaving of energy, you simultaneously recognize its sameness with everything else in life, the historical causes for it, the appropriate response and boundaries to it, and the spacious revelation of who you are, connected with all of it and yet not so at all.

twelve

other people
and places

Along our journeys of recovery and healing from addiction, it can sometimes feel very lonely.

Early recovery can feel like living in the empty space between two worlds. As if you don't have a home, and don't belong anywhere. It can also sometimes feel as though you don't have a tribe.

Loneliness, confusion, and despair may feel like constant and unwanted companions.

Can you see that the very fact of your felt loneliness, confusion, and despair is pointing to your already present, well-functioning, and healthy capacity to connect? Can you notice that while you are experiencing loneliness and despair you are also simultaneously witnessing your inherent and natural connectedness? And that it is only the smallest unseen mental rejection of loneliness that seems to transmute the starlit empty horse fields of that starved expression of connection into the apparent certain reality of a small, lonely, separate "me."

Doesn't it make sense that there are feelings of loneliness right now? After stepping outside of an addictive pattern, it does very much feel as though you are in a new world. It absolutely does feel lonely sometimes. Uncertain. Mysterious. These are not bad things.

Besides being an indicator of your ability to connect, the felt sense of loneliness is also a reflection of your strength in trusting in the possibility of a new way of being. A way of being that may not yet have materialized. If we are honest with ourselves, don't we always live in a state of not knowing? We may succeed in covering the felt experience of this over with layers of thinking, emotion, and story, but we never really know what will come next. Or if next will come at all.

With these reflections in mind, see if you can relax more when loneliness arises. Let yourself be led by wonder through the contours of its dark terrain.

From a certain perspective we are always alone.

There is no one except you who could experience the thoughts, feelings, and sensations inside you.

However, we do not exist in isolation. The people and places around us have a potent impact on our lives.

Why should we expect it to be different in recovery?

For example, although we may learn to respond to challenging situations and communications more skillfully and with more ease over time, the experience of tension in such moments remains. It is a natural human response to prefer ease to difficulty. There is nothing wrong with this. Our preference to feel good doesn't need to be transmuted or dispelled because we are in recovery from numbing ourselves from feeling bad or hurting.

It is not necessary to go to the other extreme and become a martyr, numbing yourself from your humanity. Or to become a doormat and put up with everything because "It's all in my head." It is easy to hide behind spiritual or moral ideals to avoid being intimate with the messy parts of life that scare you. You also don't need to place yourself in environments that are unhealthy "because I should be able to take it if I am really free from addiction."

Although I can go into a bar, I choose not to. I am not afraid of it. I just don't enjoy it. I don't find enjoyment in that environment anymore. If others are going to a bar to drink, I will go home and read or play music. This is my preference.

The people and places we surround ourselves with have a potent impact on our experience. In fact, they are not separate from our experience at all.

To better understand this, consider the miracle of mirage. Mirage reveals the inseparability of who we take ourselves to be and the world. For instance, you may have had the experience of driving down the road on a clear, hot summer day and seeing what looks like a puddle on the road in front of you. But when you get closer, the puddle disappears into thin air.

Scientific examination tells us that the blue in front of us was not water but sky. The hot pavement had heated the air above it enough to change its physical properties and effectively create a weak mirror. Seen from a particular angle, that mirror reflects the blue sky from above.

Isn't that amazing?!

We expect to see pavement. When we don't and something blue appears, we tell ourselves a story that fits into our assumption of the way the world should be.

We say, "Oh, there must be water there. Maybe it just rained." We actually see a puddle of water! We don't experience the blue sensation and our interpretation separately.

We see what our mind believes.

This is amazing. If we extend this further, we see that the power of thought immediately and seamlessly projects its worldview into each and every moment. Are the physical sense impression outside and mental interpretation inside even separable? Are they two things at all?

☀

Why do we habitually and compulsively add thought labels to this moment? Do we do it so that we can feel we have a handle on the way everything is? So often our lightning-quick mental interpretations of experience arise from an unconscious need to control or understand what is happening around us.

We are so mistrustful and fearful.

Even if our conscious minds do not feel that way.

The physiological, hardwired psyche is evolutionarily programmed to scan for danger. Part of this programming is to quickly assess one's surroundings for threats. The ability to label and categorize information into patterns, and fit new experience into vetted and safe frameworks we have built from past experience, plays an important role in survival. This ability has provided much that we enjoy in modern globalized society.

The categorizing mind also helps navigate the tasks of our increasingly full modern lives. However, when we are unaware of times that our inner and outer worlds are shaped by assumptions born of fear, separation, and control, these qualities unconsciously permeate our experience. Then, our inner and outer worlds take on qualities of separate, fear-driven thinking and appear to be fundamentally imbued with the sharp divisions of black and white, this and that, which unexamined mental forms of fear leave in their wake.

This process is not always overt. It can be very subtle. For instance, when we look out our window and see a "tree," exclusively as a concept rather than as a modulation of life with which we are also mysteriously connected, we are experiencing the subtle lens of unseen clenching fear. When we operate from this perspective, we feel as if we have seen it all before and what we experience is either acceptable or unacceptable.

In these moments, we have a harder time appreciating what is unfolding in front of us and an even harder time feeling that it is safe to welcome and see something in a different way. To live like this is to live trapped in a conceptual prison. Living like this, we not only reduce life to a concept, we also reduce ourselves to one.

☀

We are always experiencing mental interpretations. This is so even when we believe we are experiencing something objective outside ourselves. Recall the example of seeing water on the road on a hot summer day. In a way, whether we look inward or outward, we only ever experience ourselves.

We see that our inner thoughts—which we often think of as separate from the outer world—mix perfectly with our outer experience. The imagined water in front of us on the road is of the same essential nature as the inner thought. It is of the same essence. It is known in exactly the same way as a thought inside is known—arising within the same awareness. Our inner assumptions of the world form our so-called outer reality.

☀

Isn't this amazing?

What is equally amazing is that these inner assumptions about the way life is are also reciprocally shaped over time by life experience, and especially by relationships with others. We are always in a feedback loop where inner impacts outer and outer impacts inner. The two are of the same essential nature and are continually influencing each other.

How else could it really be?

Our relationships with others and their viewpoints impact our worldview until the two are no longer easily distinguishable.

"Outside others" can potently impact our inner experiences and shape the lens through which we behold the circumstances of our lives. This does not mean that we should reject everything and everyone we don't like.

Most of the time, it is a mix of conscious direct perception of the other person and environment and our unseen unconscious assumptions about the way that person or environment is.

Is it possible to disentangle the two? This is not a yes or no question that we can answer once and then carry with us with much effect.

It is more of a living inquiry and intimacy with life that we need to continuously reaffirm for ourselves in every moment through wonder and open curiosity.

Can you own your emotions without rejecting your sensitivity, and the impact others have upon them? For instance, if you are newly in recovery, it is pretty easy to see that being in the presence of others who are actively using is simply a bad idea. It might invite an unseen part of yourself to use again. We need to tread carefully.

Connecting with the spaciousness of this moment helps us skillfully meet challenging experiences inside and out. With that spaciousness, distinguishing what is ours, what is someone else's, and what is shared, while also feeling the presence weaving everything together as one, is possible. Resting in spacious awareness allows what is past to distinguish itself from what is present without our needing to reject any aspect of it.

You can overwhelm yourself if you go too quickly and do not feel grounded in who you are. When you are overwhelmed, and not compassionate with yourself, you can slip into autopilot. When this happens, your conditioning takes over and turns to old survival patterns. This is called relapse.

Let us tread gently. Let us familiarize ourselves with what it feels like to touch what is happening right now through the immediacy of the heart. Let us see that we need to face life but that we need to do so at our heart's pace. When we move in this way, a part of who we are may recognize that we are already home. Even if we realize that there is a huge mess that needs cleaning.

Some people I knew in AA had been there for more than thirty years. Some of them were living in daily fear of taking the next drink or drug. They were not actively using, but fear still controlled many parts of their lives and caused a lot of pain. To live free from fear—which is not the same as living in the absence of fear—we need to become intimate with what scared us so much that we felt we needed to numb out. To work with ourselves, we need both space from as well as help from others.

This does not happen in isolation.

Often, having a challenging conversation with a friend or a family member that brings up past hurt is just what is needed. If there is space to process—not necessarily with them and not necessarily then or there—your relationship to the relational pattern and, often, the relational pattern itself, cannot help but change.

How can you feel safe not feeling safe? How can you make space to feel upset, pulled, or triggered? Challenging conversations can be healing if you feel safe enough to give yourself space to feel shame and other difficult emotions and to see how natural it is to feel challenged around someone you might have had a long and challenging history with.

When you don't need to defend your point of view or accept another's point of view in order to be in relationship, there is a felt sense of freedom.

Can you share what you feel and hear what comes back without needing to make either yourself or the other person wrong?

This can be challenging.

If you are anything like me, you will likely stub your toes repeatedly. Is it possible to approach challenging communications with integrity and with the intent to heal?

After such communications, you may see eye-to-eye a little more. This can be true even without conscious acknowledgment. Amends may not have to be overtly made. However, you may find that you are both freer of resentment or anger toward each other. Your outer relationship may not necessarily be close, but this will be a choice rather than a compulsion driven by fear or anger. The decision will feel empowering rather than disempowering.

Can you see how important your relationships and communities are? Can you see that they contribute to how you feel inside? Your close relationships with others provide powerful insight into who you are. However, it is important to recognize that everyone is dealing with their own challenges and to go about exploring this living inquiry of being in relationship with another without dumping on, or unfairly relying on them, for a cathartic release.

Our relationships to the people, communities, and ecosystems that support and sustain us can enrich or degrade our life experiences. An enriching experience does not necessarily mean an easy or pleasant experience. Likewise, a degrading experience doesn't necessarily need to be challenging or abusive.

We always live in community, whether we feel isolated and alone or loved and full.

Can you see that your relationship to yourself dictates your relationship to your communities and also leads to a place where your outer environment reflects your inner one? Although this is always true, it is quite beautiful when it is consciously known and felt in the present moment. Like right now.

It is beautiful to feel that the people you meet and the experiences you have are appearing because they align with who you are and what you need.

Even if there is challenge, conflict, or disagreement.

To look at our communities and the external situations of our lives as reflections of our inner lives does not mean we overlook or condone abuse and other unhealthy behavior.

It is also not a New Age narcotic—a spiritualized heroin shot into the veins of overwhelm, trauma, and grief to take the edge off the rawness of these often natural and healthy emotional responses.

This question is intended more as an invitation to inquire into the meaning that our relationships hold. If they are here, they are not accidental. In this way, we slowly learn to approach life experience not as an obstacle to be overcome but as a welcome gift.

☀

What is it like to consider that the circumstances of our lives are gifts from life, given to learn from, relate to, and ultimately notice as distinct from our personalities but not essentially any different from who we fundamentally are?

We know ourselves to exist in the same way we know the people we are in relationship with to exist.

What is this knowing awareness that is always on?

In our simplest most direct listening, we know that who we are could never be apart from this.

Even right now while reading.

A knowing presence that is felt in the body and mind. A presence including the chair you may be sitting on. A presence including the words you are reading that are organizing into thought. That also simultaneously knows itself free of any inner or outer experience at all. An awareness that simply and indisputably is. And knows that it has always been like this.

Hosting it. Witnessing it. In the middle of it. In relationship to it. Giving life to it. And already here before any felt connection with it may appear to arise or be lost.

thirteen

learning to live with oneself again

Early in sobriety I first discovered that money had value outside the context of drugs. I had been using for so long that money had value only in terms of the amount of drugs it could buy.

This was a shocking discovery. Even though I was in the fortunate position of beginning recovery while I was in school, and during a time when I had a place to live, it was more than a little disconcerting. The value and meaning of everything else came crashing down on me. Although I had been spending a little money on the bare necessities before—food, clothes, etc.—their value had never registered.

Living with addiction is like living inside of a bubble. You can feel isolated, as though you are living in another world.

For myself, awakening to the value of money from a culturally defined perspective was an interesting and fortunate experience. For many, there is not the opportunity to awaken to the value of money in recovery. Many find themselves clean and sober for the first time while they are homeless, in prison, or without a job. But for me, entering the world of sobriety provided the space for this perspective to emerge. Everything seemed totally new. It felt easier to see at the time that money didn't really represent anything outside of the market of culturally defined values that it was created within in the first place.

Part of learning to live with oneself again is finding out for oneself what is needed to live a happy meaningful life. The set of largely unexplored collective agreements that constitute the cultural collective's recipe for happiness may or may not work for you. Learning to live with oneself again may not be easy. It certainly is not modeled well in the world we are living in right now.

The collective suite of addictions that our culture is suffering under is staggering. Our collective addictions to white supremacy, ableism, workaholism, patriarchy, and hyper-consumerism are pandemic. It is well beyond the scope of this book to do more than simply introduce this phenomena.

Simply being alive, you cannot help but be impacted by one of these addictions—either as a member of the group

actively using or as a member of the group, gender, orga-
nization, or ecosystem impacted by the addicted group's
behavior. This is not unlike the way an individual's addiction impacts that person's family, friends, and communities.

From a systems perspective, we see that the unseen pattern
of resistance to what is that births the experience of feeling
like a fundamentally separate person on an individual level
is responsible for birthing divisive forms of group identity
on a collective level.

When a group uses, it allows them to numb aspects of
their collective experience that are judged to be threatening
or unwanted. Unconsciously, the group believes that by
pushing this undesired aspect out of their daily experience,
they are erasing it from their lives. However, the rejected
experience of one group becomes the daily experience of
another. We are intimately connected with each other. In
our collective body, we cannot throw anything away. There
is no "away." Although there is momentary numbing for
one temporary modulation of life that we glibly label a
"group," the resistance to what is uncomfortable leaves a
shaky foundation. When we are controlled by addiction,
we never feel that we are safe, even when things are going
"well." There is a quiet, looming desperation and fear.

Collective resistance usually remains unseen. The addicted
group experiences this subtle layer of collective uncon-
sciousness as fact and "life as we know it."

However, just because patterns of collective resistance are
not usually felt doesn't mean they don't exist or that they

don't impact our daily experience. These seeds of collective resistance may grow into patterns of experience that we are more sensitive to— personal addiction, habitual tension in the body, or fear and anxiety that everything will fall apart if we don't stay alert and keep working. How many of us really feel safe and supported in the collective we live within?

What social addictions are you impacted by? Most of us will have more than one response. Being alive today, it is hard not to.

When feeling and releasing collective addiction within your own body, how can both the fundamental wholeness of life and the injustices and oppressions within it be simultaneously held?

How can we hold this paradox without either burning out, or numbing out?

As it expresses itself differently in each moment, we can't bring anything with us into this field of inter-being except our honesty and vulnerability. Although we also need to educate ourselves, and work to bring voices that have been silenced into the room of normalcy of whatever group we are a part of, all the knowledge in the world does little to touch the trauma in our collective body. Just as with personal addiction, where we must learn how to feel and inhabit our bodies, collectively we must learn how to have embodied conversation with others. How can we feel compassion for ourselves while doing the same for another, without dissociating from our bodies and into spiritual, psychological, or social ideologies about how we should be?

When a collective pattern of oppression or trauma is met, it feels very uncomfortable. Yet, a great deal is discovered in the process. Perhaps there is more trust in the "other." Or, you notice that the other is not really other at all, or feel a general sense of belonging that is not as tied to a particular aspect of your social identity. In the heart of inquiry into collective patterns of addiction, you may discover a sense of who you are that is not strung together with tension and resistance. This statement is not abstract: It points to a fluid, moment-by-moment discovery in the heart of present relational experience—often messy, confusing, uncomfortable, and scary.

When you can share and give voice to what is unfolding within a group on a moment-by-moment basis, and the apparent starts and stops of connection, tracking of bodily sensation, and modulations of feeling, you help mobilize collective energies of healing.

How can the words emerge from our own mouth but be breathed from collective presence? How can we attune to the presence of "we" when confronting collective addiction in ourselves?

We might call this Oneness 2.0. Both because it is a needed and likely next step in our collective healing and because it is a wholeness that includes difference, duality, conflict, and discomfort. This is a wholeness that does not require homogenized hetero-normal comfort to know itself. It is a wholeness that does not break the felt sense of connection with ourselves, those around us, and life while intimately exploring the micro and macro expressions of oppression and victimization in ourselves and our relationships with others.

Oneness doesn't segregate uncomfortable aspects of social experience from its domain of healing and love. It doesn't always need to be in comfortable surroundings, having conversations with like-minded people. In this regard, the word *politics* has been totally abused. Politics points to a deep yearning within our collective body to relate to others whom we may never personally meet. However, this privilege and beautiful human capacity for collective compassion and love has been exploited through our addiction to silencing uncomfortable aspects of collective experience—often through "divide and conquer" tactics.

Is there another way to engage politically with social structures? Can social experience be attuned to and felt in the body as a living breathing presence? Working with collective addiction in this way means deeply seeing the ways that we unconsciously form personal identities out of the social environments we find ourselves in. When we can embrace, love, and find our home in the midst of resistance around aspects of our social identities, we feel whole, yet generally uncomfortable. For instance, right now, notice the visceral responses inside your body when you receive the phrase "loving awareness." Now, how does your body respond when you receive the phrase "white supremacy"? Here, the body receives these phrases very differently. Working with our direct, moment-by-moment visceral responses in a supportive group environment allows us to gradually become aware of how larger—usually unconscious—collective patterns of addiction are manifesting in our lives.

Even if we have individually awoken to the ways we addictively formulate individual identities for ourselves that require "this" or "that" to feel okay, we also need to see how we do this collectively. Ultimately, are the two even separable?

Our preference for personal and social comfort is understandable. However, this preference becomes problematic when the so-called privileged group in a collective habitually trades in its capacity for collective compassion (literally, "to be with suffering") to remain in comfort.

How can we open wider into the relational field? It is through the presence of "we," felt in our bodies, that we can inquire most effectively into social addiction.

The presence of we does not exclude the openness that may be felt sometimes when we are sitting on a meditation cushion, or when we are in conversation with like-minded individuals. But it does not require this either. We must ask ourselves if the openness of monastic solitude is really what our heart most yearns for?

Although retreat can help us recharge so that we feel more able to breathe in concert with the leading edge of the often painful, tense, or traumatic patterns emerging from the collective body, we can also use retreat and contemplative practice as another way to numb. As Zen meditation teacher Reverend angel Kyodo williams says, "Contemplative practice is both necessary and insufficient for our liberation."

How can we learn to rest together in loving awareness, breathing as the "many made one"?

We did not consciously choose to be addicted. Many of our collective addictions were inherited through social structures that we were born into or were passed to us genetically. However, as a cell of the collective body, we each have our own share of collective addiction that we must reckon with.

You can choose to become aware of the presence of collective addiction within you. You can choose to not allow it to continue forming the background assumptions of your life that are simply taken for granted. Your liberation and healing—and that of everyone else—depend on it. The two are inseparable.

As we are living within the collective and are influenced by everyone and everything around us, our answers to what constitutes a good life for ourselves must honor both our inner wisdom and the collective outer wisdom—or lack thereof—in the culture we live within.

In the wake of stepping outside of an addictive pattern, we re-awaken to a collective we drifted away from—along with everything else—when our addictions first began. We can find ourselves in a state of open bewilderment.

This process, albeit scary, is a gift.

The psychological space often present when emerging from an addictive pattern can provide a very open space for reengaging or re-negotiating cultural standards that were left behind, ignored, or placated—but never fully embraced—while using.

This open space provides the opportunity for fundamental and deep inquiries into aspects of daily life that normally remain unquestioned. Radically honest explorations can emerge around the role that money, work, relationships, friendship, leisure time, service, race, privilege, education, and spirituality play in our individual and collective identities. This transition can provide space for a deep moral inquiry to emerge.

As you consciously re-enter this culture, one gift of addiction is your awareness that the cultural values being imposed upon you about how you should live your life are just that—cultural values. They are not necessarily your own. They don't necessarily comprise a recipe for a happy life for you.

How we make use of this newfound awareness and psychological space is what matters most. It is largely up to us whether this opportunity helps us become more self-aware, caring, loving, reflective, and individuated human beings, or whether this space is used to curl up into a ball and scream about how unfair it all is. Although the process of learning to live with ourselves again can feel very vulnerable, it is important to inquire into our relationship to vulnerability. Do we collapse into a state of victimhood, becoming more entrenched in patterns of isolation and fear, or do we dare allow our very real sense of vulnerability to connect us more with the people around us and with the mystery of this moment?

Out of the opening afforded by being thrust from one pattern into a totally new pattern of relating to oneself and the world—which can generally trail in the wake of sobriety—the possibility of discovering an inner wisdom that can help orient your decisions and directions in life becomes a real possibility. This inner wisdom may communicate, sometimes to your dismay, that you are not interested in following what society has deemed the quiet and easy path.

Are unexplored cultural prescriptions for life—for example, the culture of workaholism, the culture of hyper-consumerism, the culture of ableism, the culture of resource exploitation, the culture of white supremacy—fundamentally any different than drug addictions? They may be much more functional, and collectively they may even be celebrated. However, if cultural expectations are unquestioningly accepted to avoid feeling the fear and discomfort of facing strong, sometimes dissonant, collective energies, this behavior is fundamentally no different than other, more overt forms of addiction.

☀

When we adopt cultural beliefs about what comprises a fulfilling life without exploring the truth for ourselves personally, we do ourselves a disservice.

How often is our avoidance of our deeper motivations really a fear of feeling what makes this life unique, and of what this life is dying to express?

This is a beautiful realization. Our fear is baseless. For some reason, we have decided that we need to hide from ourselves and from who we are. Of course, we cannot ever really do this. And so, we are left with the experience of clunky fear-driven habits of mind and body. And we have mistaken them for who we are.

We have been conditioned to fearfully resist what appears new or unknown—over and over again. Just because this resistance amazingly creates the sense of a separate "I"— someone who resides behind the eyes, and who needs collective conditions to feel safe and to figure it all out— does not mean it is true. It does not mean we are actually separate or that resistance is effectively keeping us safe.

We don't need to convince ourselves of this through the perspective of the fearful separate person. Can we simply watch this process unfold within us? Can we let the experience of separateness point us toward the sensational qualities of it? You can trace the movements of sensation within and find that there is really no disconnection from the rest of the vital movements of energy within the body. You may discover that the visceral mental clenching creating the sensation of a separate me is a local expression of life. It is a beautiful expression of mirage.

The wavelike spray of sensations in the head often labeled "thought" is also present in other parts of the body. You might feel sensations of tingling in the fingers or the soothing connection with the breath that life is drawing again and again. You may relax into the calming beating of the heart that is pumping oxygenated blood throughout the body.

Is there anything personal about this? Is there a separate person in there that is in control?

You may feel through the vital sensations the movement of life energy within while simultaneously noticing the presence of that which holds all of it, including your sense of being a separate self—now more like a clenched acorn in an oak wood, than the director at center stage. And you may also discover that the noticing, too, is part of that already present wholeness.

This discovery is a letting go. Then, the spaciousness of presence and the fullness and vitality of heart beating, breath moving, hands tingling, and spray of mind moving, are somehow dancing. Life is dancing with itself.

☀

Much of what we think is good is simply what has been culturally labeled as good. There is nothing fundamentally wrong with this. However, if the collective and unconsciously agreed-upon tenets of "the good and happy life" remain unexplored, they reduce and limit our lives and who we are to a set of ideas and images.

This is heartbreaking.

I'm not saying that we should give up our jobs and go traveling around the world or something like that. We may or may not need to swing to the other end of the pendulum in order to wake up to a way of being that we find fulfilling.

The natural, creative, and spontaneous energies of life can grip us just the same as the stymied, solid, entrenched, historical energies of the cultural collective.

That being said, we often gain the perspective needed to see the relativity in any viewpoint by hanging out in another for a while. Sometimes, after ping ponging back and forth enough times, we mysteriously find ourselves free of the tension of competing perspectives.

We find that we are so much more than any pattern, energy, or culturally agreed-upon perspective.

Or any artistic driven energy.

We are the presence, space, and ground from which all of this effortlessly happens. We are the space in which all of it has already been lovingly welcomed.

In waking from one addiction, let us not fall into another. Let us not fall into the fearful collective addiction of scurrying from one thing to the next. Let us consider to what degree the squirreling away of money for the long winter—that will surely come—will actually warm us when we are in the middle of it.

In being so afraid of not knowing what might come next, and of being hurt, we have created elaborate personal, interpersonal, and societal structures about how things should be to distract us from really feeling what it is like to be intimately connected with ourselves in this moment. Which often hurts. Inescapably.

To live honestly and happily, we must live vulnerably. But this vulnerability is not gained through opening indiscriminately to being hurt. It is also certainly not found by closing off from what hurts. Vulnerability is found somewhere in the middle, tuned in to our bodies and this very breath. From letting go of the need to control this moment, we may discover something about the relationships inherent within it. Which are always changing and being redefined.

Our next action is not necessarily a prescribed one. It is not necessarily in alignment with societal values, although it very well may be. It is dictated more by the blowing winds of life. We are usually not even asking these questions when we are living like this. When we are living most honestly, there is really no other choice than the one we take. Life is making the decision. Life is moving us.

The beauty is that this life-wide decision cannot help but take into account all that you are aware of. So, please don't turn this into another conceptual framework or ideal. Please don't use this as a way to push yourself out of the picture in the service of some transcendental, bigger-than-you life trajectory that you are devoted to serving.

That is not vulnerability but a concept about vulnerability. A dissociative one. An understandable one.

It is fearful to consider what it is like to not buy into or reject cultural values. However, only through deeply honoring and seeing how natural it is to feel your fear of vulnerability and of trusting this moment can you begin to actually live more freely.

Others may not support your decisions. They may criticize your choices or label you crazy, unstable, childish, or impractical. They may tell you that you are just going through a stage and that you need to look out for your future.

This is so understandable. Others are subject to the same cultural influences you are. Historically, it has been even more unsafe than it is today to question collective values. But just as you do not need to subscribe wholly to cultural and familial values, you don't need to throw them all out, either. This life is so much more precious than any belief structure or value. This life is not a thing.

Life is always right here. In this moment. You never know what is coming next. However, your seeing and courage to feel, to welcome difficulty and fear, make all the difference in the world.

When you open yourself to this moment and trust in the intelligence of this life—the life that is beating this heart and breathing this body right now—you open to a completely different way of being in the world.

From here, although your personal beliefs are in a way irrelevant, what you express is so much more alive, impactful, and relevant than before.

※

Can you be content with a peace, security, and support that you can never bring with you anywhere? That you can never take outside of this moment and package into a thought structure? That could never belong to you or be earned? A simple seeing-being effortlessly happening right now—perhaps in the midst of struggle or discomfort. Right here, in the reading of these words.

Right now, in the midst of this reading, can you notice if a part of who you are is already free? You may notice this as a peaceful felt sense of presence that the inner and outer contents being experienced right now seem to appear within. Is there a relationship between who you are and this felt sense of presence?

As you begin to learn to live with yourself again, you will find that one of the gifts of addiction is that in taking you so far outside the cultural prescription for a good and easy life, your return to the collective provides an opening and space to deeply inquire into the truth that collective thought patterns hold for you.

With this gift, you can gradually learn to live with yourself in a deeply meaningful way—right here—in this moment. You can see that all of the planning and activity of the mind, the needs of the body, and the movements of emotion, can play out here. In this place, the value of any experience is given directly through simply being with it and seeing it fully.

You may find that the emotions, thoughts, and sensations that comprise this moment have no relevance outside their direct experience and momentary existence. Stories may develop but they tend to be less sticky. They become more inspired and loving. There is gradually less of a need to be right or look good.

Living like this, don't we go for fewer rides? Don't we gradually see that following a thought or story to the end won't really get us anywhere? Didn't we also see this with our addiction? Let us apply these lessons here. Let us see that resisting and numbing what scares us, or grasping, running after, or asking something or someone else what is good for us cannot really give anything of lasting value. It may appear to work for a while, but ultimately, just as with addiction, we find that we simply can't live that way any longer. It hurts too much.

By opening yourself to this present moment and listening in this way, you don't give up anything and you certainly don't become dumb or unable to make decisions. You may know less about what will come, but that's simply because you have gradually begun to give up the belief that time holds relevance for you outside of its appearance in this moment.

Living this way, what might you discover?

Don't you still eat when you are hungry? Don't you still process emotions when needed? Don't you use your mind as it is called for?

Living like this, you live a wilder and more present life. You see that life has less need for description or definition because both of these were requirements for a life defined solely through the lens of thought. By seeing that thought cannot provide you with lasting peace, instruction, or direction for a better life—personally or collectively—you see that who you are is so much larger.

What a gift this is.

Let us honor this gift of addiction. Let us rejoice in the possibility of the discovery of a deeply fulfilling and loving life that is always available. This is what is meant by learning to live with oneself again. Learning to live here fully.

fourteen

the gifts of addiction

It may seem strange to title a chapter of a book "The Gifts of Addiction." It might seem that these words do not belong together in the same sentence. Addiction is often considered a curse. Or something that one just barely survives. Or something that someone else didn't.

However, what if addiction is not only a condition we point to in pity, fear, or sadness, saying, "There. That is addiction." What if addiction could also be described as a totally natural, ubiquitous, evolutionary process and pattern of life?

Just as seeds grow into trees, flourish, die, and provide nourishment for a new tree to grow, the inner seeds of addiction represent a similar pattern of growth and evolution.

Life is always building on itself. The evolution of the opposable thumb and the ability to walk on two legs, for example, mark important evolutionary moments for humans.

We live in a world of constantly evolving and building patterns, where the next pattern often emerges once the previous one has been seen clearly, where the next modulation or "new" twist begins when the place of the "old" one within the greater context is understood. In scientific research, we might call this "defining the problem." When we can clearly define a problem or ask a question, we have gone far. For example, when a computer programmer sees that in order to solve a complex optimization problem they need a computer with certain specifications, a motivation for change is established. In seeing how a pattern fits into the whole, life evolves. How could it not?

When we see that a certain pattern is just that—a pattern—a new pattern that includes the old one emerges.

It is the same internally.

When we become aware that a string of thoughts, sensations, and emotions behave in almost autonomous and predictable ways and see how these patterns impact our experience of ourselves and those around us, energy naturally goes toward either amplifying and elaborating on this pattern or moving it in a different direction.

Through this process, it gradually dawns on you what you are and what you are not. To know that you are not a particular pattern of thought is freeing. If we bothered to look inward, the day for many of us would consist of a dizzying game of ping-pong, as our sense of identity bounced from one point of view and like or dislike to the next.

When you let go and realize that a trend of thinking or feeling follows a prescriptive path that can often be anticipated by those closest to you—enabling them to "push your buttons"—you realize that who you are cannot possibly be that pattern. You may not like the pattern and it may cause you and others around you discomfort, but a part of you knows it can't be who you are. Who would be there to know the pattern as a pattern if not you?

The creative, generative process of life evolution is happening all the time, moment by moment. Contents appear to emerge so that they can be seen and then slide back into the unconscious where they can serve as the foundation for a new expression of life.

From this perspective, the experiences in your life are seen as a complex web of patterns endlessly building upon and modulating themselves into new patterns.

One of the gifts of addiction is that it can wake us up to the fact that we are not a pattern at all. Often, we experience moments of clarity and can see through our behaviors or belief structures but remain convinced that we are, fundamentally, the same people we have always been. We usually feel as if "we" are here in the midst of it all, fighting to somehow make it work.

Honestly working with the energies of addiction within you opens you to the possibility of waking up and seeing that the whole sense of being a separate person fighting against life is itself a pattern. Through a conscious exploration of addiction, patterns of subjectivity and personality that are usually unconscious and unseen can be disrupted.

A gift of addiction is that the pressure of addiction can reach a level where the pattern of subject and object itself is thrown into a new light, where it can be seen that you are not who you thought you were.

Walking the path of recovery helps you see not only areas where you may have acted unskillfully and hurt yourself and those around you but also, more deeply, that the whole sense of being a separate struggling person trying desperately to make it all right is itself another pattern of life.

That there is no more or less reality to this pattern than any other, and it cannot be fundamentally who you are.

The wisdom realized through this seeing manifests as a direct and effortless letting go of the need to control and resist what is happening in this moment.

Life becomes more whole, spontaneous, and fluid, for it is seen that although there is a unique personality for which you are in part responsible, you are also much bigger and more connected than that personality could ever be. From this space, you don't need to compulsively tell stories about who you are to fill yourself up. Being here, you know that you are. You are not "this" or "that," although "this" or "that" may emerge. Simply put, you are aware.

This is the greatest gift that could be given. Addiction ultimately reveals the gift of who you are: You are the gift.

As equally in addiction, pain, and confusion as in joy, wonder, and open heartedness.

resources for
further reading

Inner Work / Psychology

o Aizenstat, Stephen. Dream tending. Sounds True, 2001.

o Eisenstein, Charles. Climate—A new story. North Atlantic Books, 2018.

o Hanson, Rick. Buddha's brain: The practical neuroscience of happiness, love, and wisdom. New Harbinger Publications, 2009.

o Johnson, Robert A. Inner work: Using dreams and active imagination for personal growth. HarperCollins, 1986.

o Masters, Robert Augustus. Emotional intimacy: A comprehensive guide for connecting with the power of your emotions. Sounds True, 2013.

o Masters, Robert Augustus. Transformation through intimacy. Revised edition: The journey toward awakened monogamy. North Atlantic Books, 2012.

o Maté, Gabor. In the realm of hungry ghosts:
   Close encounters with addiction. North Atlantic
   Books, 2011.

o Miller, Alice. The drama of the gifted child: The
   search for the true self. Basic Books, 2008.

o Whyte, David. Consolations: The solace,
   nourishment and underlying meaning of everyday
   words. Canongate Books, 2019.

Meditation / Spirituality

o Brach, Tara. True refuge: Finding peace and freedom
   in your own awakened heart. Bantam, 2012.

o Brunton, Paul. The hidden teaching beyond yoga:
   The path to self-realization and philosophic insight,
   Vol. 1. North Atlantic Books, 2015.

o Chödrön, Pema. The wisdom of no escape:
   And the path of loving-kindness. Shambhala
   Publications, 2010.

o Foster, Jeff. The deepest acceptance: Radical
   awakening in ordinary life. Sounds True, 2012.

o Kabat-Zinn, Jon. Coming to our senses: Healing
   ourselves and the world through mindfulness.
   Hachette UK, 2005.

o Kabat-Zinn, Jon, and Thich Nhat Hanh. Full
   catastrophe living: Using the wisdom of your
   body and mind to face stress, pain, and illness.
   Delta, 2009.

o   Kelly, Loch. Shift into freedom: The Science
    and practice of open-hearted awareness. Sounds
    True, 2015.

o   Packer, Toni. The wonder of presence: And
    the way of meditative inquiry. Shambhala
    Publications, 2002.

o   Rosenberg, Larry. Breath by breath: The liberating
    practice of insight meditation. Shambhala
    Publications, 2004.

o   Tolle, Eckhart. The power of now: A guide to
    spiritual enlightenment. New World Library, 2004.

o   Tolle, Eckhart. A new earth: Awakening to your life's
    purpose. Penguin Books, 2006.

o   Williams, angel Kyodo; Owens, Rod; and Syedullah,
    Jasmine. Radical dharma: Talking race, love, and
    liberation. North Atlantic Books, 2016.

Trauma

o   Blackstone, Judith. Trauma and the unbound body:
    The healing power of fundamental consciousness.
    Sounds True, 2018.

o   Heller, Laurence, and Aline LaPierre. Healing
    developmental trauma: How early trauma affects
    self-regulation, self-image, and the capacity for
    relationship. North Atlantic Books, 2012.

o   Levine, Peter A., and Ann Frederick. Waking the
    tiger: Healing trauma. North Atlantic Books, 1997.

- Menakem, Resmaa. My Grandmother's hands: Racialized trauma and the pathway to mending our hearts and bodies. Central Recovery Press, 2017.

- Porges, Stephen W. The pocket guide to the polyvagal theory: The transformative power of feeling safe. W.W. Norton & Co, 2017.

- Van der Kolk, Bessel A. The body keeps the score: Brain, mind, and body in the healing of trauma. Penguin Books, 2015.

- Wolynn, Mark. It didn't start with you: How inherited family trauma shapes who we are and how to end the cycle. Penguin, 2017.

about the author

Victor is a scientist, author, entrepreneur, and Mindfulness Based Stress Reduction facilitator. He received his PhD in Laser Physics from Cornell University. He has 10+ years of experience facilitating leadership development groups, wilderness therapy, and stress reduction courses. For more, please visit www.victorbucklew.com.

Made in the USA
Las Vegas, NV
02 December 2020

11863506R00104